LOPEZ ON GOLF

NANCY LOPEZ

WITH DON WADE

Stanley Paul

London Melbourne Auckland Johannesburg

Stanley Paul & Co. Ltd

An imprint of Century Hutchinson Ltd

62-65 Chandos Place, London WC2N 4NW

Century Hutchinson Australia (Pty) Ltd
PO Box 496, 16-22 Church Street, Hawthorn, Melbourne,
Victoria 3122

Century Hutchinson New Zealand Limited
PO Box 40-086, Glenfield, Auckland 10

Century Hutchinson South Africa (Pty) Ltd
PO Box 337, Bergvlei 2012, South Africa

First published as *Nancy Lopez's The Complete Golfer* in USA
by Contemporary Books 1987
First published in Great Britain 1988
© Nancy Lopez 1987

Printed in Great Britain by Butler and Tanner Ltd, Frome

ISBN 0 09 173689 7

Contents

To my family for all their love and support,
for all the special times we've had, and for all
the special times ahead.

Foreword

Nancy Lopez is one of the great golfers of all time. She has the charisma of Ballesteros, the ruthless, competitive edge of Jack Nicklaus and the charm and humour of Lee Trevino all rolled up into one package.

Nancy was a sensation when she first played on the LPGA tour some 10 years ago. To those of us in Britain it was pretty obvious that a superstar was in the making when we saw her in the 1976 Curtis Cup at Lytham and St Anne's. It was clear then that she had something special which was going to make her a world-beater. Nancy did for the American LPGA tour what Arnold Palmer and Jack Nicklaus had done for the men's tour. The women's tour had its great players – Mickey Wright, Kathy Whitworth and JoAnne Carner. All had been tremendous golfers, but the public in America wanted more. They wanted a television personality with the glamour and sex appeal which would bring the men out in their droves to watch women's golf. It seemed before that the outstanding golfers couldn't quite attract the galleries and television coverage which the tour needed. Those with the glamour seemed to lack that little extra personality or the exceptional golfing talent to produce what the American public wanted.

Nancy was different. She was talkative, bubbly, glamorous and good-looking, with an astonishing golf game to match. Suddenly the American public had what they wanted, with Nancy becoming the highest earner in women's sport and one of the highest paid professional golfers in the world – male or female. In 1978 she did what was unheard of before and won five tournaments in a row. Suddenly American women's professional golf was *the* sport and Nancy was very largely responsible for this. The other players on the LPGA tour had long cried out for superstars to bring them the riches and rewards of the tennis players. Some doubtless resented her emergence as the leading player, but in the main they were as thrilled as was the golfing public. JoAnne Carner, perhaps the most popular and successful of the women professionals, delighted in having Nancy to pull in the crowds. Others found the financial advantages of improved prize money and television coverage to their liking. To every golfer in America Nancy Lopez quickly became a household name and as much of a draw, if not more of a draw, than almost any of the men golfers.

Sadly the women professionals from America have a limited schedule of tournaments overseas and as such comparatively few golfers outside North America and Japan have had the thrill of seeing Nancy. She is a supreme athlete and, like Ballesteros or Nicklaus, is a player no golfer should miss seeing, given the opportunity.

This book is a great instructional book for all. It has many tips and gems of information aimed specifically at the woman golfer but has just as much to offer for every man. Nancy's way of playing golf is delightfully simple, based on a swing and technique which looks so natural that one can easily forget the hard work and practice which has obviously gone into perfecting it. Nancy hits the ball prodigious distances, distances which leave her male Pro-Am partners gaping, but as she herself explains through timing rather than strength. The book is also a delight to read for it gives an insight into the thinking and mental attitude of the world's finest woman golfer. Her positive approach, never tinged with the merest suspicion of doubt, can only lead the reader to attack the game with a new-found confidence. It is a book which I have thoroughly enjoyed reading and I am sure will enthral every other golfer.

In men's golf there are few professionals who would miss the opportunity of watching Ballesteros, Nicklaus or Palmer. In women's golf Nancy Lopez has that same attraction. Her game is an awesome one to watch and her ability to win and to keep on winning a very special talent. Combined with that she is a likeable and lovable friend to her colleagues on the LPGA tour and a devoted wife and mother to her family. Her game has literally revolutionized the women's professional scene in America. Through her, both there and around the world, there are many in women's golf whose careers and horizons have broadened considerably.

Enjoy the thoughts and theories of one of the game's all-time greats.

Vivien Saunders
St Neots, 1988

Preface

Sometimes it's hard for me to believe that 1987 was my 10th year on the LPGA tour. Ten years, and it seems like just yesterday that I was a 20-year-old rookie ready and willing to test my game and myself against the best women golfers in the world.

A lot has changed in those 10 years—to me, to the LPGA tour, and to golf in general.

Two marriages (everyone deserves a practice round), two wonderful daughters, and 35 victories later, I'm in the Hall of Fame and happier—and a whole lot busier—than I ever dreamed possible. The LPGA has grown faster than anyone expected. There are more good young players than when I joined the tour, and we're playing for much more prize money. On top of all that, I honestly believe we haven't even scratched our potential for growth.

And finally, golf itself is growing like Topsy. The "baby boom" generation has discovered what a great game it is for people of all ages. All you have to do is look at the size of the galleries on all the professional tours, and see all the young people in those galleries, and you'll know that golf is in for a very bright future.

I'm really excited by the large number of women who are taking up the game. Programs like Title IX opened the door for my generation of women to participate in all sports, and so in a sense golf is benefiting from that change. But another big factor is the number of women who have business careers and have figured out what businessmen have known for a long, long time—the golf course is a good place both to do business and to get away from the pressures of business.

After 10 years I know a lot more about myself and about golf, so it seemed like a good time to write this book.

My game hasn't changed all that much, but I understand it a little better, and that means I'll be able to share what I've learned with other golfers, whether they are beginners or scratch players, men or women.

And I really don't think I've changed that much, but I've learned a lot about setting priorities—my family, my golf, myself— and the need to find a comfortable center to balance all the demands on my time and my feelings. Sometimes this has been a hard lesson to learn, but at a time when there are an awful lot of women trying to be "superwomen," maybe my experiences over the past decade can help. I hope so.

Nancy Lopez

Introduction

Nancy Lopez and I both came to professional golf at about the same time, she as a player, I as a journalist. And while I certainly knew her as a player, it wasn't until we collaborated on this book that I began to get a sense of her as a person. The person is more impressive than the player—and the player is a Hall of Famer.

As an editor at *Golf Digest*, I've seen Nancy's highs and lows played out in a very public career. It's all there in the photographs that trace the past decade: The smiles as she put the LPGA on the map with her five straight wins in 1978. The frustration when she couldn't make the pieces of her first marriage fit. Her overwhelming love for Ray, Ashley Marie, Erinn Shea, and, of course, her sister, Delma, and father, Domingo.

Nancy is the most compelling player on the LPGA tour. To say simply that she has a God-given talent for this most maddening of games is to miss the point. As Noel Coward once observed, "Thousands of people have talent. I might just as well congratulate you on having eyes in your head. The one and only thing that counts is: Do you have staying power?"

Over the past 10 years, Nancy has proven that she has staying power. Even after reducing her playing schedule, she's still the player to watch. Anyone who doubts that need only ask the fans, the tournament sponsors, LPGA officials, or network television executives. And she's still the player to beat. She knows it, the other players know it, and the other players know she knows they know.

It is a testimony to both her confidence and her abilities that she fully expects to be in the final group on Sunday, even as she balances the demands of being a mother of two, the wife of Major League baseball star Ray Knight, and one of the most prominent athletes in the world. God knows, there are a lot of people who, faced with any *one* of these roles, couldn't get out of bed in the morning.

Working with her on this book, I had a chance to see what makes Nancy Lopez tick.

First of all, she genuinely likes herself. What you see is pretty much what you get, so she isn't burdened with the baggage of self-doubt or role playing.

Second, she genuinely likes people and derives a lot of strength from the fact that people like and admire her. That admiration is a big part of her being, since she perceived early on that she was special, and her self-image precludes rudeness, boorishness, temper tantrums, or even the hint of scandal that seems to stroll hand-in-hand with celebrities.

"Athletes have a big responsibility to the kids who look up to them," she told me. "When I see a little kid watching me, it gives me a good feeling. I know I'm a good person, and I hope that child will really want to grow up and be just like me."

Third, like all great champions she has a remarkable ability to concentrate fully on the job at hand, whether it's playing with the kids, being a wife to Ray, practicing putting, or giving yet another in a seemingly endless series of interviews. When you have her time, you have her undivided attention—and patience.

Finally, she has her family, and, golf or no golf, family has always been the center of her life. That was true when she was a kid—a phenom, if you will. It was true when she joined the tour, and it's never been truer than it is today. It is her love of family that provides a sense of stability and perspective in her very hectic and demanding world. When she was a child, her family gave her the chance to fail without being a failure. As an adult, her family gives her a chance to succeed while truly being a success.

Don Wade

Acknowledgments

Writing a book is a team effort and this book would not have been possible without the help and hard work of a lot of people. I'd like to thank them right now.

Nancy Crossman edited this book for Contemporary and did a great job under a tight deadline and a lot of pressure.

David Gibbons watched over this project for IMG, worked out hundreds of details, and kept things running smoothly from beginning to end.

Peter Johnson has been taking care of my business life at IMG for as long as I can remember, and his advice and suggestions on this book, like everything else, were invaluable.

Laura Mancine is Peter's assistant and I want to thank her for being so patient and for taking so much heat from so many people.

Nik Kleinberg brought a lot of enthusiasm and talent to the photography in this book, and who knows, maybe even came away with a better golf swing.

Penny Coyne, my "kid's keeper," helped by being with Ashley and Erinn while I worked on the book. Anyone with small children knows how much help that can be.

Of course, I want to thank Don Wade, for being both a writer and a friend and for caring about this book as much as I did.

And I want to thank my husband Ray for all the advice and support he's given me on this project and on every day of my life.

Finally, I want to thank God for blessing me with my family, my career, and my happiness.

1

Getting Started

Just as there are a lot of different ways to swing a golf club, there are as many different ways to learn how to play golf. No one method is better than the other. All that matters is the results.

Years ago, most of the top male players learned to play as caddies. All you have to do is look at the records of Sam Snead, Byron Nelson, Ben Hogan, Arnold Palmer, and Seve Ballesteros to see that this isn't a bad way to learn. Not many women learned to play as caddies, simply because until recently girls weren't allowed to caddie at most clubs. Even today, there are a lot more girls serving Big Macs at McDonald's than caddying, which is too bad.

I guess if you took a poll out on the professional tours, you'd find that most of the players took up golf because their parents were members at country clubs, and they excelled because they had plenty of opportunities to receive lessons, practice, and play in tournaments. That's the route players like Jack Nicklaus, Tom Watson, Ben Crenshaw, and Tom Kite took, so I guess it must work pretty well.

I took what's called "The Lopez Method," and naturally, it's my favorite.

I used to love to tag along with my father and mother when they played on a municipal course in Roswell, New Mexico. Dad was a pretty good player, and my mother made up in enthusiasm what she lacked in skill. In truth, I think she enjoyed being out in the fresh air with me and Dad as much as anything else.

One day, when I was eight years old, Dad took a 4-wood out of Mom's bag, handed me a tee and a ball, and told me to hit it, and hit it again, until I reached the green. He and Mom walked on ahead, and imagine their surprise when my very first golf shot went zooming over their heads!

From that moment on I was hooked, and they were hooked on my being hooked. A little later in this book, I'll talk about getting kids started in golf, but the point I want to make here is that once I took an interest, Dad gave me some simple advice and then let me learn by copying the swings and shots that I saw the better players make, while avoiding the bad swings and shots of the poorer players. That's why kids are the best students in golf. They absorb the good things without getting bogged down in a lot of theories.

Too often golf instruction sounds like the directions for building a lunar lander. Here is the sum total of what my father taught me about the fundamentals of the golf swing:

"Nancy," he said, "bring the club up real slow; bring it up real high; extend your arms real far; hit the ball right on the sweet spot, and send it into the middle of the fairway. Then just keep hitting it until it's in the hole."

Nothing too cosmic there, but the funny thing is, the simpler I keep things, the better I play. Try to keep that in mind, especially if you are just taking up the game. Trust your instincts. Find a swing that feels comfortable and works for you and then practice until you can groove that swing. If you try to remember all the theories, and take all the advice people will try to give you, your brain may suffer a golf meltdown.

THE RIGHT EQUIPMENT

Buying golf equipment is one of those "good news, bad news" situations. The good news is that equipment will last a long time if you take good care of it. The bad news is that it can be expensive.

Clubs: Which Ones Do You Really Need?

The *Rules of Golf* say that you are allowed to carry 14 clubs. They don't say that you *have* to carry 14, so right from the start, let's talk about which clubs you really need.

I play with Northwestern clubs. I carry a driver, a 3-wood, 4-wood, the 2- to 9-irons, a pitching wedge, a sand wedge, and a putter. Some players carry a 5-wood in place of a 2-iron, since they feel the 5-wood is easier to hit and will carry the ball roughly the same distance. Other players carry a 1-iron instead of a 4-wood, because the 1-iron will hit the ball on a lower trajectory, which is better in the wind. Still others will leave out a long iron (a 1-, 2-, or 3-iron) and carry a third wedge with increased loft. This club is good for those delicate little pitch shots around the greens.

The point is, all golfers have the option of choosing the clubs they feel best suit their game and the course they will be playing. The right equipment can make all the difference in the world. It can make the game easier and a lot more fun, which is the whole point of playing.

If you are just beginning and are not even sure you're going to like golf, here's my best piece of advice: don't even invest in a set of clubs. Instead, if you are going to take lessons from a professional, ask if you can borrow a 5- or 6-iron that fits your body type, strength, and swing. It just doesn't make sense to invest several hundred dollars in clubs that are destined to spend the next five years collecting dust in your basement.

Once you decide you really like golf—as I know you will—you can think about buying clubs. Let's run through the bag and talk a little bit about what you're going to need.

Driver. A lot of people recommend that beginners forget about hitting the driver. It has the longest shaft and the least amount of loft, and that can make it intimidating and difficult to hit. I see their point, but I think one of the real thrills in golf is hitting a driver right on the screws and watching the ball sail off down the fairway. I would recommend getting a driver with a small head, which will be less intimidating. Also make sure it has plenty of loft—at least 12 degrees.

A key to picking the right driver—and all the other clubs—is making sure it looks good to you. It's important to feel comfortable and confident out on the course, and looking at a bagful of ugly clubs isn't going to do much to raise your confidence level.

Here's another rule: don't even think about buying a club until you've hit several balls with it. It may look great, but if you can't hit it, how good is it? Any respectable golf professional will be happy to let you try a club on the practice tee, and in fact, many companies supply the professional with "demo" sets just for that reason.

One last thought on buying a driver. In the last few years metalwoods have become very popular, and almost every major company makes them. Since they are basically hollow, the weight of the clubhead is distributed around the outside, or perimeter, of the clubhead. Many people feel this allows them to hit the ball straighter.

I've been playing with a metalwood recently, and while I like it very much, I'm still looking for a driver with a head made from persimmon, a very hard wood. I learned to play with persimmon woods, and they just feel best to me. As I said before, feel is very important in this game, and especially important to me.

Fairway Woods. The 3-, 4-, and 5-woods are important, especially for shorter hitters, because they will be used often. I often suggest that beginners hold off on trying a 3-wood because I think it is a very difficult club to hit. True, it does have more loft than a driver, but it's a difficult club to hit off the fairway. People have a tendency to try to scoop the ball into the air with a 3-wood, and that creates all kinds of problems in their swings. As far as I'm concerned, for beginners a 3-wood is just a nice place to put a headcover.

The 4-wood, on the other hand, is a great club. It has a nice small head and plenty of loft, so it's easy to get the ball into the air. It's also a good club for hitting shots out of the rough, because the clubhead will slide through the heavy grass without twisting off line the way an iron can.

I also think a 5-wood is a good club, for a number of reasons. First, it's a good club for beginners because it gets the ball into the air so easily. This really builds confidence quickly. Second, it's a good club to have in your bag if you play on a course that either has a lot of rough or has greens that require high, soft approach shots.

Quite often, players in national championships like the U.S. Open or U.S. Amateur will replace their 2-irons with 5-woods just for that reason. A number of companies make 5-woods with especially heavy soleplates, and some even build little runners onto those soleplates. These clubs are really good for getting the ball out of the rough.

To be honest, I think the majority of golfers I see would be better off if they swallowed their pride, admitted that they can't really hit a 2-iron, and replaced it with a 5-wood. The game is tough enough without kidding yourself, right?

Irons. Remember what I said earlier about finding a driver that looks good to you? That's even truer when it comes to irons because there are many more of them to look at.

Right here I have to make a confession. If you look in my bag you'll see that I use a mix of new clubs (long and medium irons) and a few favorites from an old set of clubs I used earlier in my career. Those old short irons just look good to me, and I play so well with them that I haven't been able to replace them.

You might be surprised by just how many touring professionals and top amateurs mix up their bags the way I do. It's because golf is a game of such personal tastes and feel. For example, a lot of players have switched from conventional forged blades like those I play to more radical designs such as the cast irons, which they feel are more forgiving of slightly mis-hit shots. These cast irons are literally cast in a mold and are designed to be more forgiving on off-center hits. Forged irons are ground into the proper shape, but their traditional design will not compensate for mis-hit shots.

Now, I say where there's smoke there's usually fire, and if that many good players use cast clubs, there must be something to the new designs. But for me, they just don't look right, and I've never been able to play them. That doesn't make them bad clubs, but they aren't the clubs for me.

At any rate, whether you choose traditional forged blades or the new cast irons, there are a few things you ought to keep in mind.

First, I think most players, and certainly most beginners, would be better off with irons that have a fairly wide and slightly rounded sole (the part of the iron that rests on the grass when you address the ball). This design is a little more forgiving when shots are mis-hit.

I also think that most players would be better off with irons that are slightly offset. That means the leading edge of the iron is set back slightly behind the hosel of the club. This design makes the club easier to hit properly because it presets your hands slightly ahead of the ball.

You also want to be certain that the irons have the right lie. That is, you want to check to see that when you set the clubhead behind the ball it sits squarely on the ground. A good way to check this is to assume your address position while standing on a floor or another firm surface. Once you've done this, have a friend check to see if the sole of the iron is resting fairly flush with the ground. If there is space from the toe of the club into the center of the blade, the clubs may be too upright for you; if there's space between the heel and center of the blade, the clubs may be too flat. Either way, a professional can check for certain and make the needed adjustments.

Once you settle on a set of irons, it's a good idea to have a professional check to make sure each individual club has the correct degree of loft. Quality control at the manufacturers is pretty good, but it doesn't make any sense to spend good money on a set of clubs, only to find out that the reason you keep sailing shots over greens is that you're the proud owner of a bag of 2-irons.

If you are realistic, I think the smart move would be to try to buy a set of irons that doesn't include any long irons. They are just too difficult for beginners and many mid- to high handicappers to hit. As Lee Trevino once joked, a 1-iron is a good club to carry in a thunderstorm because "even the Good Lord himself can't hit a 1-iron." By the way, Lee doesn't even try. He carries a 4-wood.

Sand Wedge. There probably isn't a shot in golf that scares the majority of players more than a bunker shot. But it wouldn't, if they would only invest in a good sand wedge.

A sand wedge is designed to glide through the sand and under the ball. As it does, the sand throws the ball out. The clubhead should never touch the ball. Unlike a pitching wedge, a sand wedge has a wide flange. More important, the trailing edge of the flange is lower than the leading edge. The combination of the width of the flange and the difference between the leading and trailing edges of the flange is known as *bounce*. The more bounce a sand wedge has, the easier it is to play shots from the sand.

So far, so good. But it does get a little complicated. A wedge with a lot of bounce is a good club in very fine, soft sand. As a general rule, however, playing from firm sand calls for a wedge with a slightly narrower sole and less bounce.

You also need to consider what other shots you plan to hit with your sand wedge. Many—in fact, most—good players use their sand wedges for all kinds of shots from 75 yards in and around the greens. For a sand wedge to serve also as a good pitching club, it must have a narrower flange and less bounce. A sand wedge that can do both jobs is difficult to find, which is one reason players rank a good sand club, along with a good putter and driver, among the three most important clubs for scoring.

Specialty Wedges. Since a club that works as a sand wedge and pitching club is so difficult to find, in recent years most manufacturers have been making specialty, or 60-degree, wedges. Unlike traditional sand wedges, which have 57 degrees of loft and varying degrees of bounce, these specialty wedges have more loft and very little bounce. These clubs are adequate out of bunkers but are designed primarily for delicate little shots around the green and for pitch shots with a lot of backspin.

Since by now I hope I've convinced you to forget or at least hold off on playing with long irons, I think it might be worth your while to consider adding one of these third wedges to your bag once you become comfortable with the mechanics of the short game.

Putter. The most personal club in the bag is the putter. It has to look good to you. It has to feel just right. And you absolutely have to have confidence in it because, more than any other part of the game, putting demands total confidence.

I use the same putter I've used since I came on tour, an old mallet that I like because it is a little on the heavy side and I feel the extra weight makes it easier for me to put a smooth, easy stroke on the ball.

Some people switch putters depending on the speed of the greens, going to either a heavier or lighter putter on faster greens. I don't think that's such a good idea. Once you've found a putter you trust, stay with it. If the greens get super fast, experiment with striking the ball off the toe of the club. I find that this compensates for the increased speed of the greens, while allowing me to make my regular stroke.

My one firm suggestion is to make sure you select a putter that has enough loft to get the ball rolling smoothly. If a putter doesn't have enough loft, the ball will skid coming off the putter. This attention to loft is especially important if you putt on slow or rough greens.

I also think that many players might benefit from trying a putter that has extra weight out toward the heel and toe, since this will help compensate for putts that aren't hit quite squarely or on the sweet spot. I've also discovered that putters with a slightly longer blade are easier to aim and therefore help give you a little more confidence that you have the right line.

Grips

There are three basic grip materials—rubber, leather, and rubber with cord material blended into the rubber. Of the three, I suggest rubber for the majority of players. It's easy to maintain. All it takes is an occasional cleaning with warm water to restore the original tackiness.

Leather grips are fine, and they do give many players a better sense of tackiness and feel, but they are difficult to maintain because they become hard and slick very easily.

Cord grips—and there are a variety of grips with different degrees of cord in them—are fine, especially in hot, humid weather. The problem is that unless you have very tough skin they can literally rub you raw. Unless you play a great deal of golf, cord grips probably aren't for you.

A factor that is often overlooked is grip size. The smaller your hands, the smaller you want your grip. A good rule of thumb is that when you grip the club, you want the fingertips of your left hand to just barely touch the palm of the left hand. If your grips are too small, you will tend to hook the ball because your hands will move too quickly through the hitting area. If your grips are too big, you'll tend to slice or block a lot of shots because your hands won't be able to release properly at impact.

One final thought about grips. If you suffer from arthritis, ask your professional about installing some special oversized grips. In a lot of cases, these grips can make a world of difference.

Shafts

We've talked a lot about how important it is that a club look good to you, but perhaps the single most critical element in putting together a set of clubs is making sure you have the right shaft. You can have the best swing in the world, but if you have to play with shafts that are either too stiff or too flexible, you don't have a chance.

There are no hard and fast rules defining proper shaft flex. In many respects, it's a trial-and-error process for even the best players. Still, here are some guidelines:

The stiffer the shaft, the straighter you will hit the ball. However, a shaft that is too stiff will cause you to lose distance and leave the majority of your shots out to the right because the clubface will not square up at impact.

The softer or whippier a shaft, the more it will tend to increase distance. The problem is, if a shaft is too soft, the clubhead will be difficult to control and the ball will tend to hook out of control.

I use a men's regular shaft in my clubs. So do most women on the LPGA tour. Most male professionals and top amateurs use a stiff shaft, with a fair number playing extra-stiff shafts. I guess the best rule of thumb is, the more clubhead speed you can produce, the stiffer the shafts you need in your clubs. This is one area where the advice of a good professional can really come in handy.

Balls

I play with a 100-compression balata ball. If you are a beginner, that might not mean too much to you. Here's what it all means. A 100-compression ball requires more clubhead speed to compress than a 90-compression ball. I think I can spin a 100-compression ball better than a 90, but there are an awful lot of good players who feel that just the opposite is true, so for me it again comes down to feel, and I just prefer the feel of the 100-compression ball.

Balata is a natural material that the ball's cover is made from, and pretty much everyone agrees that it is easier to spin the ball if it has a balata cover. In addition, it is a softer cover than the synthetic materials that cover other types of balls. This is important when it comes to hitting approach shots that will check up on the green, when you are trying to fade or draw the ball, and when you are trying to hit it high.

The ball I play is also a wound ball, which means that under the cover are hundreds of yards of elastic windings, wrapped tightly to form a core. A wound ball will also spin better than a ball with a solid core.

Now that I've told you why I play the ball I do, let me tell you one very good, commonsense reason why you shouldn't: wound balata balls cut very easily, and even if you don't cut them, the covers get scratched and nicked, and the balls get knocked out of round after several holes. Golf balls are expensive. I get mine for free, but you probably have to pay for yours.

All that should be reason enough for the huge majority of golfers to play solid balls. They don't cut. They don't get knocked out of shape. They don't cost any more than wound balls and last a whole lot longer. Trust me.

The Bag

Now that you have an idea of what clubs and balls you need, let's spend a second on what you should carry them in. First, you want a solid, well-made bag that will stand up to punishment and also balance easily and comfortably. Unless you travel a lot, you probably don't need a big bag. If you do, it's a good investment since it will help prevent your clubs from getting mangled. Along those lines, it's also good to have a cover that will fit over your entire bag.

Check to make sure that your bag has a cover that fits over the clubheads. This will protect them in travel and also help keep them dry in case of rain. Also make sure the bag has several good-sized pockets, including a pocket large enough to include a rain suit or at least a windbreaker.

It's also a good idea to get a bag with a wide, well-padded strap. Even if you aren't planning to carry it yourself, take pity on the poor kid who will carry it for you.

One last tip on buying a bag. Check to make sure that, if you are supposed to get a set of clubhead covers with the bag, you get them. They go a long way toward keeping your woods looking new, but there's no sense in paying for something twice.

In the Bag. A big part of playing good golf centers on being prepared for anything. To do this, often all it takes is a little planning when you pack your golf bag. Here's what I carry for a tournament: extra balls, usually a half-dozen; tees; ball markers; lip protection, such as Blistex; sun block; adhesive bandages; athletic tape; bug repellent; lotion to keep my skin from cracking; at least four gloves; a rain suit or windbreaker; an extra towel; a visor or hat; club cover; a copy of the *Rules of Golf*; extra shoelaces; raisins, dried fruit, and peanut butter crackers for quick energy. I never eat candy bars, usually because I'm in the middle of a diet, but also because the sugar is tough on my nerves.

Shoes

I think a good pair of golf shoes should be sturdy but comfortable. I don't think they should be heavy, but they must be solid enough to bear up under the strains of walking, swinging, and playing from uneven lies. It's also a good idea to check to make sure that their spikes are plenty long. It doesn't do much good to try to play on a set of nubs.

Lopez File: JoAnne Carner

JoAnne is easily one of the greatest female golfers in history. She holds the women's record for winning the most USGA national championship titles, and when I was coming along as an amateur she was my idol.

I just love JoAnne's attitude. She is a very intense competitor, yet she never lets a bad shot get to her. In fact, the more trouble she's in, the better she seems to play, and I think that's one sign of a true champion. She has a lot of heart.

We've gone head-to-head in the final group several times, and I've enjoyed it. As a player, you want to know you've beaten the best, and when you're playing against JoAnne, that's what you have to do. I know she wants to win as much as I do, but whenever we're paired together, she always says something like "Let's go out and show them we can play." And we usually do. I think we bring out the best in each other's game.

I remember one incident in particular that illustrates just how JoAnne can motivate me—although she probably wishes she hadn't motivated me quite as much as she did.

Going into the final round of the 1978 Golden Lights tournament outside New York City, I was a couple of shots back of JoAnne, who was leading the tournament. I was in the middle of my five-in-a-row win streak, and there was a lot of attention and pressure on me. I picked up a paper Sunday morning and read a quote that got my attention. JoAnne said she was going to leave me in the dust. I know she meant it as a joke, but even though I didn't say anything to anybody, I promised myself that if anyone was going to be left in the dust, it wasn't going to be me.

I was in the group just ahead of JoAnne, and I started birdie-birdie, checking after each hole to make sure JoAnne was paying attention. She was. When the day was over, I had shot a smooth little 65 for myself, and I won by two shots.

Later, in the pressroom, JoAnne was great about the whole thing.

"I guess Nancy left me in the dust," she laughed.

JoAnne's suffered from back problems for the past few years and was sick much of last season. Those are two reasons she hasn't won as often as before, but another reason is the way the LPGA sets up the courses for our tournaments.

They set up the courses too short. I've complained about this before, and so have JoAnne and many of the other players. As it stands now, week after week the LPGA is putting on a putting contest instead of a golf tournament. Golf is supposed to reward power and accuracy off the tee and shotmaking with every club in the bag. As it stands now, we don't do that.

As for what you can learn from JoAnne's game, I guess the best thing is her attitude. She plays one shot at a time and doesn't let a tough break get to her. There are a lot of talented golfers on the tour who should win based on skill but can't control their emotions or temper. If there was a two-stroke penalty for temporary insanity, they might never break 100. JoAnne's just the opposite. She's always in control—of her emotions and her game.

2

The Fundamentals

As I wrote earlier, there are a lot of variations in the golf swing. My swing doesn't look like JoAnne Carner's, and neither of our swings will ever be confused with Mickey Wright's. And I don't recall anyone ever saying how much Lee Trevino's swing reminds them of Sam Snead's.

One thing all good players have in common, though, is sound fundamentals. True, you can play with a bad grip, incorrect address position, poor ball position, or a lightning-fast tempo. The problem is, playing with poor fundamentals is like driving a car with loose wheels. Eventually the wheels are going to fall off. The only question is when.

On the following pages we'll run through the key fundamentals that will give you a fighting chance at building a golf swing that will not only work, but will work time after time. I have to warn you in advance, though, that mastering the fundamentals takes hard work. Developing a good grip or a sound stance takes patience and concentration—two qualities it helps to have if you hope to play good golf.

THE GRIP
The Most Important Fundamental

If I had a magic wand that would let me change just one thing in most of the golfers I see in pro-ams or outings, it would be their grips. Ninety-five percent of the amateurs I see have grips that won't let them improve. They can hit practice balls until they faint from exhaustion, and it won't do a bit of good. They can take lessons, read books, watch videotapes, and even go through hypnosis, but until they get a good grip, they are doomed to mediocrity—if they can even get that good.

Why is the grip so important? Your hands are the only part of your body that actually control the golf club. The best swing in the world won't hold up under the gun if you have a bad grip.

I believe there are three basic keys to a good grip, and I'd like to go over them before we get into the actual mechanics of gripping the club.

First, your hands must work together. One hand cannot dominate the other. I think of my left hand as the "control" hand and my right hand as the "power" hand. I can hit the ball as hard as I want with my right hand, as long as my left hand controls the hitting action. We'll get into this in more detail in the chapter on shotmaking.

Second, your hands must grip the club so that the clubface can hit the ball squarely time after time. I take special care to make sure that the palm of my right hand is parallel with the clubface. I know that doing this means that when my hand is square to the ball at impact, so is the clubface. I don't have to try to manipulate the clubface back to a square position if my right palm is going to square it up for me. I also try to grip the club so that the back of my left hand is parallel to the clubface and my right palm. This way my hands can work together.

Finally, I want to grip the club just tightly enough to control it but not so tightly that I lose feel or that tension builds in my hands, arms, and upper body. Sam Snead says he grips the club just like he'd hold a little bird—tightly enough to control the bird, but not tightly enough to crush it. I like to think of gripping the club with the same pressure I'd use to hold a tube of toothpaste that isn't capped—tightly enough to hold it, but not so tightly that the toothpaste comes squirting out all over the place.

Left Hand: The Control Hand

One key to a good grip is to hold the club in the fingers as much as possible. Your fingers have more strength and more feel than your palm, so doesn't it make sense to take advantage of that?

My left-hand grip has the club running across the knuckle of my forefinger and the butt end of the club pressed against the muscular pad at the base of my palm.

When I close my hand over the grip, the V formed by my thumb and forefinger should point somewhere between my neck and right shoulder if I set the club down in an address position. If the V points to the left of my neck, the grip will be too weak and I won't be able either to control the club during the swing or to hit the ball squarely. Most often, a weak hand position like this will result in shots that slice weakly to the right. If the V points too far to the right, the clubface will be closed down at impact, and the result will be some of the ugliest low hooks in golf history—unless you compensate and produce a lot of blocked shots to the right. Either way, it won't be pretty.

Right Hand: The Power Hand

It's a funny thing, but most people can get their left hand on the club without much problem. It's the right hand that gives them fits. In most cases, people will get their hand turned way under the club because they feel this will give them more power and control. Believe me, it doesn't. I know because it was the way I used to grip the club until it kept getting me in trouble.

As I mentioned earlier, it is crucial—I can't stress this enough—that the right hand be placed on the club so that the palm and the clubface are parallel. I want to insure that both the clubface and the palm of my right hand are square to the ball. Here are two tips I got from 1964 U.S. Open champion Ken Venturi that will help you learn the proper right-hand grip:

First, hold your hand out as though you were aiming an imaginary pistol. Now, with your left hand holding the club in front of you, just keep your right hand in that "pistol position" and apply it to the club, closing your hand gently around the grip. Easy, right?

This second tip will help give you a feel for grip pressure, as well as helping you take advantage of the feel you have in your thumb and forefinger.

Holding on to the club with just your right hand, grip it as you

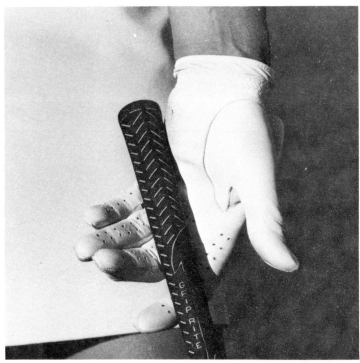

The key to a good grip with the left hand is holding the club in the fingers, not the palm. Ideally, the back of your left hand should be parallel with the palm of your right hand.

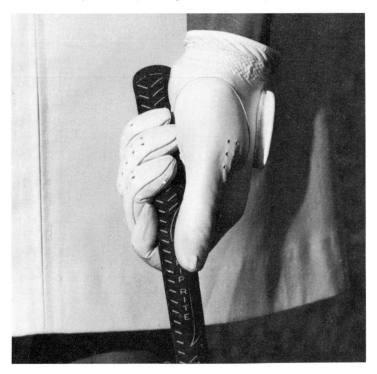

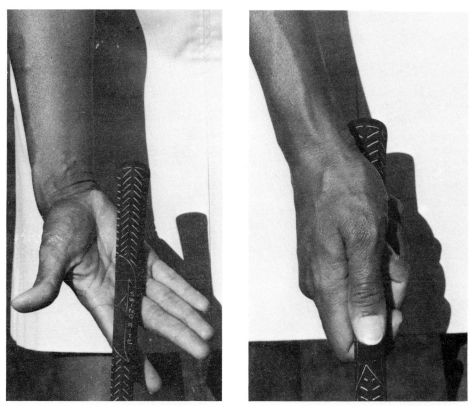

I grip the club with the fingers of my right hand, and constantly check to make sure the palm of my right hand is aligned with the clubface. This makes it easier to return the clubhead squarely to the ball at impact.

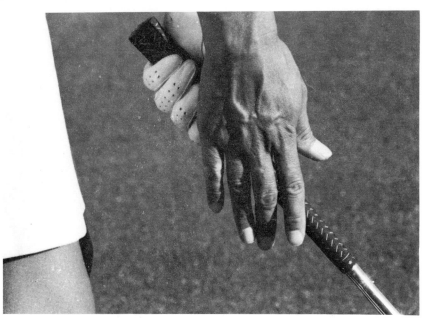

would a fishing pole, with the thumb and forefinger forming a hook. Now just pretend you're casting flies out there after a trout. Nice and loose, plenty of easy, flowing motion in your hand and wrist. Piece of cake.

The Finished Product: Putting Everything Together

There are three basic grips: the Vardon or overlapping grip, the interlocking grip, and the 10-finger or baseball grip. The grip you choose is totally a matter of individual feel.

I use an interlocking grip because, even though I have big hands, it's always felt the most comfortable. A number of fine male players also use this grip, including Jack Nicklaus and Tom Kite. Usually this grip is recommended for players with small or weak hands, but not necessarily—again, I think it's a matter of feel.

In this grip, you simply set the little finger of your right hand in the space between the forefinger and middle finger of your left hand. I think this is really a good grip for beginners because it gets their hands working together easily.

The Vardon or overlapping grip is probably the most popular

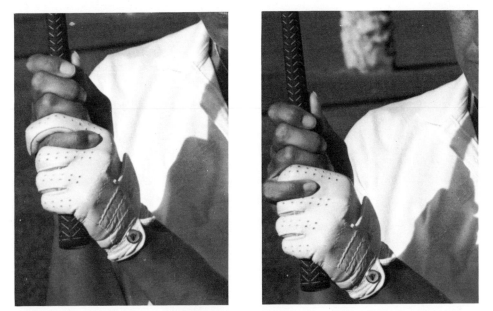

There are three basic grips: The interlocking, where the little finger of the right hand and the forefinger of the left hand are interlocked; the Vardon or overlapping grip, where the little finger of the right hand overlaps the left hand; and the 10-finger or baseball grip, where both hands are completely on the club.

grip. In this grip, you set the little finger of your right hand over the notch formed between your forefinger and middle finger of the left hand. Many people make the mistake of actually lapping the little finger over the forefinger, but I don't think the hands work together as well in this position.

The 10-finger grip isn't used much anymore, although players like Bob Rosburg and Art Wall certainly play very well with it. Actually, one time when I was a kid I jammed my finger playing dodgeball and had to play with a 10-finger grip. I played pretty well with it, too.

I think a 10-finger grip is a good one for kids because it gets all their fingers on the club. This gives them a little more control and power. It's also a good grip for older people who've lost some strength over the years.

Whichever grip you choose, the idea is to position your hands together on the club so that they complement each other.

I suggest gripping the club with your left hand first, then aligning your right hand so the palm is parallel to the clubface. When you put your right hand on the club, line up your left thumb so that it fits along the lines that run along the base of your thumb pad. Then slowly and gently close your hands around the grip, getting as much of the grip in your fingers as possible, and don't forget to let the grip rest in the hook formed by your right thumb and forefinger.

It takes time, patience, and practice to develop a good grip. If you are serious about it, have a grip put on a cut-down shaft and then

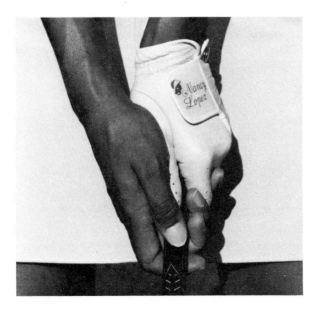

A good grip allows your hands to work together as a unit. You want to grip the club tightly enough to control it, but not so tight that you feel tension in your arms.

practice gripping the club as you watch television or do other things that leave your hands free. The more you practice, the more natural and comfortable it will feel, and the better it will work.

One last thought about the grip. The best players—and especially the best short-game players—have all had very strong hands. If your hands are a little on the weak side, I think it would be a good idea to do some exercises. Squeezing a tennis ball is good, and so is using those little grippers or hand springs that you squeeze together. Ray uses them all the time when he's driving around. It makes me crazy, but it also makes him stronger, so you can guess who wins out.

THE STANCE
A Base to Build a Swing On

One of the keys to a sound, successful golf swing is balance. There are very few good players who get out of balance in their swing, and even fewer poor players who stay in balance during theirs. A proper stance can go a long way toward ensuring that you will remain in balance throughout your swing.

For years, people have been told that they should address the ball with their feet shoulder width apart, but that's confusing. Does it mean that the outside of your feet should be shoulder width apart, or should you stand so that the inside of your feet are shoulder width apart? See what I mean?

I have a better suggestion. I tell people to set their feet just outside their hips. In other words, if you drew imaginary lines from the outside of your hips to the outside of your feet, those lines would be farther apart at the bottom than at the top.

This stance width rule will give you a good guideline, but depending on how you are built, you might need either a slightly wider or narrower stance. Here's a drill to help you determine just how wide your stance should be.

On the practice tee, select an iron you feel comfortable with. A 5-iron is usually a good choice. Begin by hitting nice, easy shots with your feet close together—almost touching for the first few shots. Once you've warmed up, begin hitting the shots a little more firmly. As you do, you'll find that you need to widen your stance to support the increased speed and motion of your swing. Keep this up until you are making your normal, full swing. At the same time, keep widening your stance until, eventually, the wider stance restricts you from making a nice, full turn with your hips and upper body. Once that happens, you know you've gone too far, so return to a slightly narrower stance, and you'll be in business.

A good rule of thumb is that your stance should be wide enough to support your swing, but not wide enough to restrict it. Also, keep in mind that your stance width will vary slightly from club to club. For example, my stance will be wider for my driver than for my 5-iron, simply because the force of the swing for a driver requires more support from my lower body.

There's one other misconception I'd like to clear up about the stance. People have always been told they should have a square stance, which is fine. The problem is that people think this means their feet should be square—or parallel—to each other and perfectly perpendicular to the target line. This won't give you the base you need.

To give yourself the best stance, your left foot should toe out slightly to the left while your right foot remains perpendicular to the target line. In fact, if you find it difficult to make a good turn on the backswing, you might even experiment with toeing your right foot out just a little. This will make it easier for your hips and upper body to turn.

BALL POSITION
The Forgotten Key

There are two schools of thought concerning ball position. One school holds that every shot should be played from the same ball position. The other teaches that the ball should be played off your left heel with a driver and then moved back to the right slightly as the clubs get shorter.

By and large, I'm a believer in a constant ball position because that's how I learned to play and it makes the most sense to me. Also, I see so many players struggle as they try to play consistent golf from inconsistent ball positions.

The truth is, your ball position determines your swing because every element of your swing, from how you address the ball to how you actually hit it, is based on where the ball is positioned in your stance. If you have a poor ball position, or if you vary your ball position, what are your chances of playing good golf? Not very good, I'm afraid.

I play virtually all my full shots off my left heel. I move the ball back slightly—and I stress *slightly*—with middle and short irons, only because these clubs must be hit with a descending blow, rather than the more sweeping motion needed with a driver, fairway wood, or long iron.

The only time I drastically alter my ball position is when I'm trying to hit a specific shot. For example, if I want to hit a high fade or slice, I'll move the ball forward in my stance; for a low draw or hook, or a knockdown shot, I'll move the ball back toward the center of my stance, since this will hood—or deloft—the club, allowing me to hit the ball lower.

All too often, I see players who have the ball back in their stance complain that they can't get the ball into the air. They try to solve this by flicking at the ball, trying to scoop it into the air. If they would only play the ball up off their left heel, they'd solve their problem. The one thing that's true about golf is that it's a game of cause and effect, and once you learn to spot the causes, it becomes easier to correct the effects.

Addressing the Ball—5-Iron. At address, I position the ball forward in my stance. I rarely vary my ball position unless I want to hit an especially high or low shot. Notice how freely my arms hang, and how close my hands are to my body. Too often, people make the mistake of reaching for the ball and get out of position.

AT ADDRESS
Ready to Play

Ben Hogan once said that, as far as he was concerned, once he studied a shot, selected a club, and addressed the ball, a golf shot was 90 percent over. That says a lot for how much he trusted his swing, but it also says something for how crucial a good address position is for every golfer.

A proper address position allows you to aim the club properly. It allows you to make a solid, repeating swing in balance. It puts you in a position to hit any kind of shot you want and, maybe most important of all, it puts your mind at ease, giving you the confidence to swing away.

A little later, in the shotmaking chapter, we'll go into the variations at address that will allow you to hit different shots, but for right now I want to talk about an address position that will help you hit one straight shot after another. That wouldn't be too tough to take, would it?

My most important consideration when addressing the ball is that the clubface be aimed exactly at my target. Everything else I do is keyed to this. To do this, I've developed a preshot routine that I follow for every shot, from the longest drive to the shortest putt.

I begin by studying the shot from behind the ball. I visualize exactly how I want the ball to fly. In my mind's eye, I can literally see the entire shot, from beginning to end. I try to imagine how the swing is going to feel, from the slow, smooth move away from the ball, to setting the club at the top, to firing down and through the ball to a nice, high finish. All this may sound funny to you, but almost every top player I know does this for every shot.

As I stand behind the ball, my eyes trace an imaginary line running from the target through the ball. I look for a spot on that line some four to six inches in front of the ball. Usually it will be a piece of grass that's a different color from the rest.

As I walk into the ball, my only consideration is setting the clubface perfectly square with that intermediate target. I'm not concerned about the real target right now—just that piece of grass a few inches away.

Once I'm sure that my clubface is square with the target, I carefully put my right hand on the grip, making sure that the palm of

**Addressing the Ball—
Driver.** Compare this
position with my address
position with an iron, and
you can see that I play
the ball further forward in
my stance. This is because
I want to sweep the ball
off the tee with a driver,
rather than hit down on
the ball as I do with an
iron. Also, notice that my
hands remain close to my
body and my arms hang
freely.

my right hand is square with the clubface and facing a point parallel to the left of my target.

Now that I've gripped the club, I build my stance, being very careful not to either open or close the clubface. I set my feet, making sure that they are on an imaginary line that parallels the target line. Unless I'm trying to fade or draw the shot, I want my feet parallel to the target line.

When I'm hitting a straight shot, I make sure that everything is lined up squarely with the target line. My eyes, shoulders, and knees are all square with the target line. People often talk about keeping your hips square, but if your knees are square with the line, your hips have to be square, too.

People often seem confused about how far from the ball they should stand. More often than not, I see people bending from the waist and reaching for the ball, because this feels like a more powerful position. In truth, it's a position guaranteed to leave you lunging out of balance every time.

My rule is that you want your arms to be able to hang freely from your shoulders so that you can make a nice, easy swing around your body. When you address the ball, you should be able to pass your right hand between you and the butt end of the club. If you can't do that, you're probably too close to the ball. If there's extra space there, you're too far away, but the odds are about 99 to 1 that you'll be too far from the ball more often than you'll be too close.

I stand fairly tall at the ball, but I still have a comfortable amount of flex in my knees. Like any other athletic movement, you need to have some flex in your knees to help support your weight and the motion of the swing.

While I may have a little less knee flex than other players, the key point is that I maintain that flex throughout my swing. This keeps my swing on a consistent plane. The ball is hard enough to hit without bobbing up and down all over the place.

A pretty good rule of thumb is to flex your knees at address at about the same degree that you'd flex them if you were going to dive into a pool. Your weight should be balanced in the middle of your feet, and sticking out your fanny a little will help you stay in balance.

One final bit of advice on addressing the ball. The vast majority of golfers, including the really good ones, tend to miss shots to the right. It's Mother Nature's fault. As we stand over a shot or a putt,

Pre-Shot Routine. All good players have a routine they use to prepare for a shot. They do this on every shot. My routine is simple, and a good one for you to copy. I study the shot from behind the ball, visualizing exactly how I want the ball to fly. Then I approach the ball from the side, setting the blade squarely behind the ball, taking care to make sure it's aligned with an intermediate target on the line between my ball and the target.

there's a tendency to aim our bodies at the target, rather than remembering that it's the club that should be aimed at the target, while our bodies are aimed at a not too distant spot that is parallel to the left of the target. If you find that you're missing a lot of shots to the right—including putts—keep that in mind and compensate for it. I think you'll like the results.

Once I set the blade, I place my right hand on the club, and check that the back of my left hand, the palm of my right hand, and the clubface,

TWO FUNDAMENTAL MYTHS

Almost everyone who has ever played golf has heard these two "rules":

"Keep your left arm straight" and "Keep your head still."

In theory, both of these rules make sense. The problem I have with them is that they result in a lot of unnecessary tension in the golf swing—and tension is a killer in golf.

A straight left arm is fine as long as you don't confuse straight with stiff, which is what I see a lot of people doing. I would rather see people playing with a softer, more relaxed left arm, even if that means it gives a little bit on the backswing.

Maintaining a straight left arm can help if you have a tendency

are all aligned squarely. Then I set my feet, and take one last look at the target.

to overswing, but a better solution is to practice making three-quarter swings with a short iron. Don't make the mistake of making the swings faster just because they are shorter. Try to maintain a good tempo, and I think you'll find that what you think is a three-quarter swing is really getting the club back to parallel at the top of your backswing—which is just where you want to be.

If you studied sequence photographs of the great players, I think you'd be surprised by how many of them move their heads laterally in the golf swing. That's because the swing is, at least to some degree, a sliding as well as a turning motion. Very, very few players move their heads up and down during the swing, which is why maintaining a consistent knee flex is so important.

Instead of stressing keeping your head still, I'd rather emphasize how important it is to focus on the ball until it is gone. The old saying "Keep your eye on the ball" is good advice for all sports, but it's particularly important in golf. Just for the fun of it, watch some of your friends hit shots and notice how often they close their eyes prior to impact, particularly with the longer clubs.

Maybe it's an instinctive reaction, but just try to hit some shots with your eyes closed, and you'll see how difficult it becomes.

So rather than tell people to keep their head still, I tell them to focus very hard on the ball. I actually try to see the clubhead hit the ball. It's surprising how much better they hit it and how still they keep their heads without thinking about it.

TEMPO
Putting the Fundamentals to Music

There is no one right tempo for everyone. I have a very slow, deliberate tempo in my golf swing that suits my personality. When I'm playing in a tournament, I like to give myself plenty of time to get to the course, warm up, and get myself mentally ready to play. If I have to hurry, I have a hard time getting into the swing of things.

A player like Tom Watson is just the opposite. If he tried to swing with my tempo, he might not break 80, and I promise you, if I tried to play at his breakneck speed, there's no doubt that I wouldn't break 80—I'd self-destruct before I finished the front nine.

I think that, within reason, a slower tempo works best for most people because it gives them time to coordinate their swing. I know that when I've laid off for a while, I have a tendency to swing faster than normal, and when that happens I tend to get anxious and jump at the ball from the top of my swing.

My first rule concerning tempo is that you should be able to feel where the club is at all times. If you swing too fast, you have a tendency to grip the club for dear life, and that destroys your feel. I like to be able to feel the club swinging back and setting into the "slot" at the top of my backswing. From there, I'm in position to go ahead and hit the ball.

One thought about the swing that I've had since I was a kid is to take the clubhead away slow and low to the ground. I literally think, low and slow, low and slow. I know that if I do this I will keep the clubface aligned to the target, rather than jerking it open if I pull the club inside the target line too early on the backswing. This also sets the pace for my entire swing. It's like a governor on an engine.

Here are a few tips that will help you develop a nice, smooth tempo. You'll know when you've found the right tempo—it will show up in your shots.

The Two-Ball Drill

Find a nice, level place on the practice tee. Tee up a ball and then put another ball down on the ground behind it, along the target line. Using a driver—since this is the club that demands the best tempo—address the ball. Then begin your backswing, pushing the second ball away with the head of the driver. If you are taking the club back low and slow, the ball should roll straight back away from your target.

The ball you hit should fly long and straight, right toward your target. Once you get the hang of this, practice it long and hard until the feeling is ingrained in your muscle memory bank. Once you've done that, try hitting your other clubs, using the same tempo and the same takeaway. Just remember, slow and low, slow and low.

Swing to a Count

Sometimes it helps if you count your way through the swing. As you address the ball, count alone, "One, two, three." Then swing to that count, setting the club at the top of your backswing on "one," hitting the ball on "two," and holding your follow-through on "three."

Play a Mind Game

When people think of a beautiful golf swing, invariably they think of Sam Snead. His swing is still a picture of graceful, flowing power and finesse. His great rival, Ben Hogan, swung the club at a much faster pace, and whenever he and Sam were paired together Sam made it a point not to watch Hogan's swing, for fear that unconsciously his swing would get faster and his timing would be destroyed.

I know I love to play with people who have a tempo similar to mine, since it helps my timing. It might help you if you have a mental image of someone with a good tempo like Sam Snead. Think about that swing, almost as though you were playing a movie through your mind. Actually imagine how it might feel to swing at that speed, then go ahead and match it with your practice swing.

Sing a Simple Song

I've always loved music, and while I don't usually hum or sing to myself on the course, when I'm playing my best I do seem to have a certain rhythm to my swing and game. If you have a problem finding the right tempo, why not try humming or running a tune through your head. Nothing too fast, mind you. Just something with a nice flow. Maybe a waltz or something like that. Sometimes a piece of music will get you through an entire round. In fact, I know players who have a lucky song and are very superstitious about it.

One final thought about tempo: I find it very difficult to play good golf when I'm riding in a golf cart. I find that walking gives me time to compose myself between shots. I get to cool off if I've hit a bad shot or calm down if I've hit a good one.

More important, though, walking is crucial when I'm trying to maintain a good tempo. I find that if I can walk a little more slowly, it's easier for me to slow down my swing. If I'm racing to the ball in a cart, talking with someone and bouncing all over the place, it probably will cost me a half-dozen shots a round. I just can't concentrate, and my timing is shot.

Golf is a relatively painless way to get essential exercise, especially for older people. Why not take advantage of it by walking whenever possible? Who knows? It may benefit your handicap as much as your heart.

Lopez File: Amy Alcott

Photo courtesy of Robert Walker

Out on tour we call her "Amy Adversity," and there's nobody who is better when the pressure is on and the conditions are awful. She won the 1980 U.S. Women's Open at Richland C.C. in Nashville in unbelievable heat and humidity. Not only did she win, but she finished four under par, nine shots better than Hollis Stacy, who finished second.

Amy is just a year older than me, so we've known each other since our junior golf days. Even then, she impressed me as being a very tenacious competitor and one of the best pure shotmakers I've ever seen. You cannot hide a pin from Amy, and the tighter and more demanding the course, the better it is for Amy.

Amy is an exciting player to watch because she is so aggressive. She just goes out and attacks the course, and that makes her fun to play with. There's never a dull moment when she's around—both on and off the course—and I think she genuinely loves to play and enjoys the challenge of competition.

One thing I really admire about Amy is her ability to keep things in perspective. She's been a star on tour since she came out as a kid in 1975, but she's able to separate Amy Alcott the golfer from Amy Alcott the person. That's not always easy to do when you're in the public eye.

She's also very generous with her time. She gives as much of her time to charities as anyone out here, and she's always willing to go out of her way to help promote both the tour and individual tournaments.

Amy is the most consistent player on our tour, and she might well be the most consistent player in all of professional golf. She's won 26 official events, and while she's never been the top-ranked, dominant player out here, she's won at least one tournament every year since joining the tour, including three out of our four majors.

If Amy has a weakness in her game, it's that she doesn't think she's a good putter. Confidence counts for a lot in golf; and it counts for a whole lot on the greens. It's a funny thing, but over the years a lot of the outstanding shotmakers didn't regard themselves as good putters. Ben Hogan even said once that there are two games—golf and putting. I think Amy kind of feels the same way, but nobody wins as much as she has without being able to get the ball in the hole.

If there's one thing you can learn from Amy's game, it's her ability to concentrate, no matter what is going on around her. She just believes she's stronger than any adversary, whether that adversary is the course, the weather, or her opponents. When you watch Amy Alcott play, you know that, while she might not win, she's not going to beat herself—and you can bet she's going to go out with both guns blazing.

3

Shotmaking: The Fun Begins

I've always enjoyed learning to hit a wide variety of golf shots, and I really admire players who fit the shot they want to play to the shape of the hole and the playing conditions. Once you've mastered the fundamentals of the golf swing, this is an area where you can really improve if you are willing to put in some hard work. It's also an area that can help you save strokes when you are faced with difficult playing conditions such as strong winds or tricky pin positions.

Many of the best shotmakers in golf are players who learned to play with just a few clubs. Seve Ballesteros, for example, learned to play with just a 3-iron. This forced him to learn to improvise, and even today, if you put him out on a course with just one club, he'll still be able to turn in a score right around par.

The key to this sort of versatility is understanding some fundamentals about the swing and about what makes balls fly the way they do when hit in a certain manner. Experienced players do this almost by instinct. It's almost as though their eyes see a certain situation, their brain programs the proper shot, and their muscles produce the shot.

In this chapter, I want to give you the fundamentals of shotmaking that will allow your muscles to hit the shots the course and playing conditions require. When you can do that, you'll have taken a giant step closer to becoming a complete golfer.

Full Swing (face on). As you study these pictures, I hope you can get a sense of the length and flow of my golf swing. I concentrate on taking the club back in "one piece." That is, I don't cock my wrists until my hands are waist high. After setting the club at the top of my swing, my

hips slide left, and my right elbow tucks closely to my right hip. This delivers the club to the ball on the correct inside path. I extend my arms fully toward the target following impact, and reach for the sky, making a nice high finish.

Full Swing (side view). From this view, you can see how I take the club straight back from the ball. This helps me keep the blade on line throughout the swing. My hands are nice and high at the top of my swing which helps ensure a nice, big swing arc and more clubhead speed. Notice that my knees remain flexed, and that my head is level

through the swing. Coming into impact my right elbow is tucked closely to my right hip, and you can see that this helps me hit the ball from the inside. My long, high follow-through shows that I have fully released the club at impact.

DRAW VERSUS FADE: WHICH IS BEST FOR YOU?

I like to draw the ball, or hit it slightly from right to left, for the majority of the shots I play. I think the draw is a stronger, more aggressive shot, and it's the swing and the ball flight I feel most comfortable with.

There are times, however, when I need to fade the ball, or hit it slightly from left to right. For one thing, a fade will not run as far as a draw because it doesn't have as much overspin. This makes it a better shot if you are trying to drive the ball into a narrow fairway landing area. It's also a better shot to hit to a tight pin placement because it will stop more quickly on the green.

The key to hitting these shots, along with the expanded versions of these shots—the hook and the slice—is knowing not only how to hit them, but how much the ball will move when you try to work it. This is where practice becomes so important. It doesn't do you much good to throw a beautiful little cut shot in at a pin, only to watch it balloon into a slice that leaves you in a bunker with no chance of getting up and down to save par.

Hitting a Draw

Earlier, in the section on fundamentals, I discussed the importance of a proper stance and ball position. These elements are particularly important when you try to work the ball one way or the other.

To draw the ball, look at a spot on the back right-hand quarter of the ball and hit it at that spot. Use the ball's trademark in that position to guide you.

To draw the ball, or hit it from right to left, I want to make sure that I hit the ball with the clubhead moving from inside the target line, to square at impact, to back inside the target line.

The best way I know to ensure this inside swing path is to address the ball with a slightly closed stance. I address the ball with the square stance I described earlier in the book, and then simply drop my right foot back off the target line. In other words, if you drew a line from my right toe to my left toe, that line would point to the right of the target if I was playing from a closed stance. By doing this, I make it possible to strike the ball from the inside, and give it a right-to-left spin.

Very often, I see people alter their grip to try to draw or hook the ball. They will turn the left hand to the right, into a "stronger" position. I disagree with this method because it simply complicates matters. Stay with your basic grip and simply alter your stance. It also helps if you move the ball back slightly in your stance. Again, you'll have to experiment to find the ball position that will allow you to fade or hook the ball best but I strongly suggest that you not move it farther back than the middle of your stance, since the farther back you move the ball, the more you are inclined to hood the clubface. The combination of a hooded clubface and a closed stance will produce some of the worst-looking duck hooks you'll ever see.

As I've mentioned before, feel is a very important factor in playing golf, and that's especially true when it comes to shotmaking.

To put a right-to-left spin on the ball, you want the toe of the clubhead to come into the ball ahead of the heel. In other words, you want to have the clubface closing down at impact. To do this, your right hand must pass over the left at impact. The more the clubface closes down at impact, the more spin you'll be able to put on the ball and the more the shot will fly from right to left. To get this kind of hand action in the swing, it helps if you think of being very "wristy" at address. As you waggle the clubhead at address, let your hands and wrists feel very loose and make sure you have a nice light grip pressure on the club.

In terms of actually hitting the shot, you want to try to take the clubhead away from the ball farther inside the target line than you would for a normal shot. Don't hurry the swing, which is a natural tendency, but let your hands release fully at impact. Again, you want them to feel very loose. It will also help if you look at a spot on the back left-hand quarter of the ball and try to hit the ball on that spot. In fact, if you are hitting a tee shot or are on the practice tee, you

Drawing the Ball. To hit the ball from right to left, I set up with a closed stance, which allows me to aim to the right of my intended target.

I take the club back inside the target line, and then drive down and through the ball, with my right hand releasing fully at impact. This allows the toe of the club to turn over, putting a right-to-left spin on the ball.

Drawing the Ball (side view). To hit a draw, I set up with a closed stance and aim to the right of my target. I take the club back inside the line and, after setting the club at the top of my swing, concentrate on releasing the club freely at impact. My right hand crosses over my left, which causes the toe of the club to turn over, putting the proper spin on the ball. I don't change the pace of my swing, just the shape of my swing.

might try putting the trademark in that position and then try hitting the ball squarely on the trademark. This will help you swing into the ball from the inside.

As in all shots, it helps if you visualize the flight of the ball as you address the shot. Burn the image into your mind, and when you make your practice swing, get a feel for how the swing you need to make will feel—and for a draw or hook, it should feel very loose and relaxed.

One final thought: a ball hit from right to left will run, and the more spin you put on it, the farther it will run. Take that into account when you study the shot. It doesn't help to crack a big draw off the tee, only to watch it bound through the fairway and into trouble. It will also fly somewhat lower, which makes it a good shot when you need to drive the ball into the wind.

Hitting a Fade

Occasionally logic and common sense really do come into play in golf, and this is one of those times. To fade or slice the ball, you do just the opposite of what you do to bring it from right to left. Let's run through the important points one by one, comparing them to the previous section on hitting a draw or hook.

Stance. Again, this is the most important alteration I make when I want to hit the ball from left to right. I play this shot from an open stance. My feet, knees, and shoulders are all aligned to a point well left of my target. This allows me to strike the ball with an outside,

To fade the ball, move the ball slightly forward and keep the clubface open at impact.

to on the line, to inside swing path. This path sets the clubface open at impact and produces a left-to-right spin on the ball.

Grip. While I don't change my grip, I do alter my grip pressure slightly. I grip the club a little more tightly in my left hand. This will keep my left hand from breaking down at impact and will help keep the clubface slightly open at impact. The more open the clubface is at impact, the greater the amount of spin put on the ball.

Ball Position. To hit a fade, I move the ball slightly forward in my stance. Again, just as in other shots, you have to experiment to find out which position works best for your swing.

The Swing. As I've said, the key to this shot is keeping the clubface open at impact. To do this, I take the club away from the ball, trying to move it outside the target line. This will cause me actually to swing on a slightly more upright plane and will help me cut across the ball with an open clubface at impact. You must consciously keep a firm grip with your left hand, not letting the right hand cross over the left until well after impact.

If you are having difficulty visualizing how this swing should look, my suggestion is to watch Lee Trevino play sometime. Actually, he doesn't fade the ball as much as people think, but his swing is designed to fade the ball at will. He takes the club back outside the line, then drives down and through the ball while keeping a firm left wrist. The ball comes out nice and high and lands softly. The beauty of his game is that he takes virtually all the trouble on the left side out of any hole he plays. That's a big edge.

Keep in mind that a fade or slice will fly higher than other shots and will run less. That's important to remember when planning a shot, because you may need to take one more club to reach your target if you plan to hit a fade.

Fading the Ball. To hit the ball from left-to-right, I set up to the ball with an open stance. My left foot is pulled back from the target line, which allows me to aim to the left of my target. I take the club back outside the target line, and at impact I keep my left wrist firm. This keeps the clubface open at impact, and puts the proper left-to-right spin on the ball.

Fading the Ball (side view). I open my stance at address, pulling my left foot back off the target line. I aim left of the target and take the club back outside the target line. At impact, I try to keep my left wrist from breaking down and allowing the right hand to take over. I want to keep my left hand and wrist firm at impact, and keep the clubface open through impact, putting a left-to-right spin on the ball. My key thought is to take the club back outside the line, and then return to impact along the same swing path.

HITTING IT LOW
The "Knockdown" Shot

There are a lot of times in the course of a round when being able to knock the ball down is a valuable shot to have. It's good in the wind, because the ball will drive lower and be less influenced by it. When you study players from Texas or the British Isles, where the wind is a big factor in the game, you quickly see that they are all good at hitting the ball low and out of the wind.

It's also a good shot if you've hit the ball in trouble and have to hit a low shot under branches and limbs. And it's the shot to play if you find your ball sitting in a divot mark.

The two keys to this shot are weight distribution and ball position.

You want to play the shot from either a square or closed stance, depending on how low you need to keep the ball and how far you want it to run. A closed stance will tend to cause a right-to-left shot that will run. Either way, you want the majority of your weight set on your left side, both at address and throughout the shot. There's scarcely any weight shift in this shot.

The ball should be positioned back in your stance, at least to the middle of your stance and possibly even more than that. Keep in mind, however, that the more you move the ball back in your stance, the more you deloft the club you plan to hit.

With the ball back in your stance, you will automatically find that your hands are set well ahead of the ball. This is where you want them to be at impact as well, and you'll find this is an easier shot to hit if you have a slightly firmer grip pressure, since it's essentially a "hit and hold" shot.

Take the club back straight away from the ball and remember that this is a three-quarter swing. You just want to set the club at the top of your backswing—your hands should be about shoulder height—and then drive down on the ball with a descending blow, with your hands leading the clubhead into the hitting area. All you are doing is "punching" down on the ball. Your left wrist doesn't collapse, and your hands don't release. Just punch down on the ball and hold your follow-through.

The mistake most people make with this shot is trying to hit it too hard. Remember that the harder you hit the shot, the more spin you'll put on the ball, and you'll actually cause the ball to fly higher than you want. It's a three-quarter shot, played with a three-quarter swing at three-quarter speed—and it will run, so make sure to take that into account when you plan the shot.

Hitting the Low Shot. When I need to hit the ball low, I play the ball back in my stance. At impact, my hands are slightly ahead of the ball, which takes loft off the club and allows me to hit the ball lower.

HITTING HIGH SHOTS

Being able to hit the ball high can help you recover from trouble. Trust me: it's a lot easier to hit a ball over trees than it is to hit a ball through them.

A high, soft shot is also good when you need to land the ball softly on the green. If a ball is going to stop, you need either height or spin, and there are some circumstances that simply won't allow you to spin the ball.

Again, just as in hitting the low shot, the important points are weight distribution and ball position, and, in addition, swing shape.

Your weight should be set so that most of your weight is on your right side. The ball should be positioned slightly forward in your stance, toward a point just off your left foot; your hands should be set behind the ball at address; and you want to grip the club very lightly.

I also think it's a good idea to open slightly both your stance and the blade of the club, since this combination will serve to increase the loft of the club at impact and help you hit the ball higher. It will also make the shot fly from left to right, so keep that in mind.

To hit the shot, I take the club away from the ball with a quick wrist break, taking the club away slightly outside the target line. I want to feel that I am sliding the club under the ball at impact and then "reaching for the sky" on my follow-through. In effect, I'm making a swing that is shaped almost like a U—my backswing and follow-through are very steep, but my angle of approach at impact is very shallow. Again, I try to slide the clubface under the ball.

It's important that you have a good lie to try to hit this shot. If a ball is sitting down in the grass, you run the risk of blading the shot. It's also important to remember that the higher you hit the ball, the more distance you'll be giving up. The force of the swing is being used to create height, not distance.

One final thought: unless you have a sand club without much bounce, it's better to hit this high, soft shot with a pitching wedge, particularly if you open the blade to increase the effective loft of the club.

As I've tried to stress, you really need to practice these shots to find out what works—and what works best—for you. A fun way to practice these shots is to play "Call Shots." It's like the game "Horse" that people use to practice shots in basketball.

The idea is that your opponent—and you can have as many people playing as you want—calls a shot he or she plans to hit. Say a high fade with a 5-iron. If the player hits the target with the shot, everyone else must pull off the shot or lose a point. At the end of the game, the losers pay up.

The reason I like this game is that it forces you to concentrate instead of just beating balls off into the distance. It also teaches you to hit the shots under pressure, and that will pay off when you try to hit these shots in competition.

Lopez File: Pat Bradley

Photo courtesy of Robert Walker.

There's been a lot of talk this year about my "rivalry" with Pat since she had such an outstanding season last year. She was easily the tour's dominant player, as evidenced by her winning three of our major championships. I honestly believe she deserved more attention as a possible "Golfer of the Year," but, of course, you could make a pretty strong argument for Greg Norman.

The truth is, Pat has had a great year coming for a long time. I'd like to believe that if I had been out there last year I might have made a pretty good showing myself, but that's not meant to belittle what Pat accomplished. She's a competitor, and so am I, and to the extent that we both want to win every time we tee it up, sure, I guess we have a rivalry.

The strength in Pat's game is in her long irons. She's so strong and has such a good swing that she can hit these clubs that give so many other golfers fits. If you are as strong and talented as Pat Bradley, keep the long irons in your bag. If not, give them a heave.

I think people misunderstand Pat. She's very friendly, and I like her very much. But on the course she's very stoical. She doesn't show much emotion, and she grinds on every shot. That's how she plays her best golf. If she tried to be like JoAnne Carner, it would be very difficult for her. I know she wants the galleries to like her— gosh, don't we all?—but it's difficult for her to reach out to them.

Pat is very serious. She takes everything to heart, and I think that being the way she is actually delayed her breaking through. She seemed to agonize over not winning more, and because she's such a private, reserved person, it was hard for her to release that pressure. After a while, that begins to eat away at your confidence, and I think that happened to Pat.

In a sense, now she has a bigger challenge to face. As tough as it is to get to the top, it's even harder to stay there. That's true in any sport, as I've learned from watching Ray last year. There are more demands on your time for interviews, outings, endorsements, and charitable work. This must be especially true for someone as private as Pat.

When you've had the kind of year Pat Bradley had in 1986, the question on everyone's lips is, "What can you do this year?" That can be a hard question to answer . . . and it's a harder expectation to live up to.

I think one reason Pat finally broke through is that she learned to become a little less intense. I think that's a lesson that can help an awful lot of golfers. So often I see players who are so tense and wound up that I keep waiting for them to vaporize right before my eyes.

Look, you just cannot play if you are that tense. Your muscles won't function, and your nerves can't cope. Give yourself a break. Relax. Take a deep breath, play one shot at a time, and be thankful you are lucky enough to be where you are, at least for a few hours.

4

Around the Greens

One of the biggest differences between weekend golfers and the top amateurs and professionals is their respective approaches to practice.

The weekend player will spend hours on the practice tee belting ball after ball down the range—that is, if he or she bothers to practice at all.

The really good players spend at least as much time working on their short games—chipping, pitching, putting, and mastering bunker shots—as they do on their full swing. They know that a good short game can mean the difference between a good round and a great round and, maybe more important, the difference between an awful round and an acceptable one.

If you want to prove to yourself how important your short game is, try this test next time you play: After each hole, record the number of shots you took from around the green. Include in that number all the shots you took from 50 yards or so off the green. After your round, break down that list, and I think you'll find that, depending on your handicap, between two-thirds and three-quarters of your shots were taken around the greens.

If that's the case, just think what even a small improvement in your scoring shots would mean to your handicap! And believe me, this is one area where everyone is equal. Big, strong long hitters don't have an edge around the greens. It all comes down to skill, experience, confidence, and, most of all, practice.

I think that if you are realistic, a good practice routine would be to divide up your practice time according to the shotmaking chart I just described. If two-thirds of your shots are taken around the greens, then two-thirds of your practice time should be spent working on those shots.

PUTTING
Where Confidence Really Counts

Putting is the most individualistic part of the game. While it is true that all good putters have a few things in common, for the most part, everyone is at least a little different in his or her approach to putting.

As I've said many times earlier in this book, I think that feel counts for almost everything in golf, and that's especially important on the greens. It's very hard to have a good feel for a putt if you are uncomfortable over the ball, so my first rule is to find a putter and a stance that let you feel relaxed and comfortable.

In Chapter 1, we talked about finding a good putter. I'd like to run through that one more time.

I think you should find a putter that is heavy enough for you to feel the clubhead, but not so heavy that it requires you to put a death grip on the club to control it.

I think it should look good to you. There are a lot of good players making a lot of putts with putters so ugly I wouldn't keep one in the trunk of my car, but those putters look good to them.

A good putter will also have a face that makes it easy for you to align the putter squarely to the hole. You simply cannot make a confident stroke if you're unsure where the putter is aimed. Inevitably you'll pull or push the putt in trying to compensate for the misalignment—either real or imagined.

There are all kinds of putter grips available, and I'd suggest you experiment to find the one that's most comfortable for you. You want a grip that allows your hands to work together as one unit. If you find a putter you like but it has a grip that feels uncomfortable, a professional can put a new grip on in a few minutes. It's surprising what a difference that can make.

I think you should pay some attention to the way the putter rests on the green. You want a putter that sits fairly flush with the ground, without much space under either the heel or the toe of the putter. Keep in mind that a fairly flat lie on a putter will tend to encourage a wristier stroke, while a more upright putter will encourage more of an arm-and-shoulder stroke.

Finally, I think people often overlook the length of the shaft. If a putter is too short, you'll become uncomfortable bending over the putt; if it's too long, there's a tendency to feel that you don't have control over the stroke.

Grip

While there are three basic ways to grip a golf club for a full shot, there are all sorts of ways to grip a putter—interlocking, overlapping, reverse overlapping, cross-handed, 10-finger, split-handed, and so on and on.

I use the same interlocking grip that I use for my full swing. The only difference is that I run my right forefinger down the grip. I think this gives me a little better feel and control over the stroke. Craig Stadler grips his putter the same way, and he has been a good putter for a long time. I noticed recently that Seve Ballesteros also extends his finger down the grip, but not quite to the same degree as Craig or I do.

Just as I do for my full shots, I want to make sure that the palm of my right hand is square with the blade of the putter. Running my finger down the grip helps ensure this. My left hand is placed on the putter so that the back of my left hand is square with both the putter blade and the palm of my right hand.

I think this is an important point, no matter what kind of grip you use. Almost every good putter makes sure that his or her hands work together as a unit. Jack Nicklaus turns his left hand well under the shaft, but he turns his right hand under the grip to the same degree. Tom Watson turns his left hand more on top of the grip, then complements it by setting his right hand on top of the grip, too.

I think grip pressure is also important. I grip the putter just tightly enough to control it. I want to be able to feel the putterhead during the stroke. So very often people become tense over a putt, and that tension shows up in their grip. You won't make many putts with the tense, jerky stroke that a death grip produces.

Finally, people seem confused about whether they should wear a golf glove while putting. I don't, because I have a much better feel without a glove. A lot of very good putters keep their glove on to putt, so like everything else, it all comes down to what feels best to you.

Stance

I putt from a square stance because I believe that an open or closed stance will create complications and require compensations, and my whole approach to golf is to keep it as simple as possible.

Still, there are a lot of very good putters who putt from a slightly open stance. Jack Nicklaus is probably the best example. An open stance helps many people see the line of the putt more easily, and it clears the left leg and hip out of the way of the stroke.

There have never been very many good putters who had a closed stance. The late Bobby Locke was one, but then he liked to hook every shot he hit, and that made him a big exception to the rule. I think that a closed stance magnifies the tendency most of us have to aim to the right of the target. After all, if you aim right and then close your stance, it's not going to help the ball roll to the hole, unless you make some alterations in your stroke—and that many calculations and compensations would lead me to a migraine, not to mention some awful putting rounds. I'll stick with my square stance.

Ball Position

As I do for most of my full shots, I like to play the ball off my left heel. Any farther forward, and I tend to hit the ball on the upstroke; any farther back in my stance, and I'll hit down on the ball. Either way, the ball will bounce for the first foot or so of the putt, the time when you want it to be rolling smoothly toward the hole.

Just as big a consideration is where the ball rests relative to your eyes. Ideally, you want your eyes right over the ball, and you want them parallel to the target line. You can get by with your eyes inside the target line, but if your eyes are outside the line, there's a tendency either to pull your putts to the right or to cut across them with an open blade, actually slicing them to the right.

The Stroke

Years ago, most players used a "jabbing" putting stroke. They were very wristy putters who made a short, punchy stroke with very little follow-through. This was an effective stroke on the slower, bumpier greens of that era.

Today the greens are faster and smoother, especially on the professional tours and the better courses. As the greens have become truer and quicker, the putting stroke has evolved into a longer, smoother stroke controlled by the big muscles of the arms and shoulders. These muscles are less likely to become twitchy under pressure.

I like to think of my stroke as "brushing" the ball. I have very little wrist break, unless it's a long putt that requires a little more clubhead speed. Mine is a very long, unhurried stroke. In that respect, it's sort of a mini-copy of my full swing.

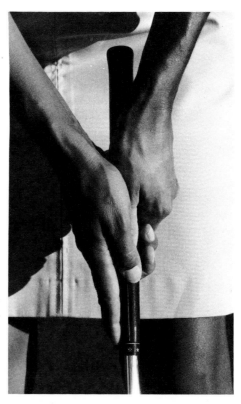

The Putting Grip. Feel is the key to putting, and to a good putting grip. I use an interlocking grip, and just as in my full swing grip, I make sure the back of my left hand, the palm of my right hand, and the blade of the putter are all aligned squarely. I also run my right forefinger down the grip for better feel and control.

When I was a kid, I would cut all my putts, hitting them with an open blade and putting a left-to-right spin on the ball. I was a good putter with this method, but it required that I aim well left of the target. It added a variable that I couldn't always gauge correctly, and I knew that eventually putting like this would break down and cause problems.

Now I work very hard to align the putter with the target, then I take the putter away "low and slow" and accelerate through the ball. My stroke is just long enough to hit the ball the right distance. Too often, I see players take a long backstroke, then try to slow the putter down at impact. This deceleration almost always sends the ball off line.

After impact, my thought is to keep the putter moving toward the target. I try very hard not to look up until well after the ball is gone. In fact, on some short putts I'll just look at the spot where the ball was until I hear the ball drop into the cup.

Reading Greens

Right here seems like a good spot to make an important point. Most people three-putt, not because they misread the break, but because

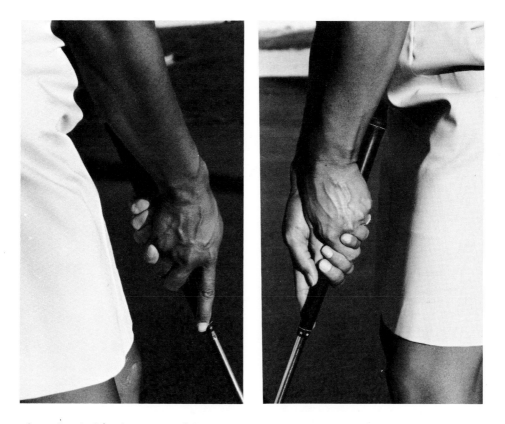

they don't hit the putt with the correct speed. Think how often you've either left a putt well short of the hole or run it well past. In either case, how well you read the putt is irrelevant because you either never got the ball to the hole or hit the ball so hard you putted it right through the break.

The rule is, worry about the speed first, then concern yourself with the break.

Reading a green actually begins as you approach the green. You can get a pretty good indication of how the balls are going to break from the overall contour of the green, as well as the surroundings. Putts will generally break away from the mountains and toward any bodies of water.

Once you reach your ball, study the putt from behind the ball. You might also look at it from the low side—that is, from the side the putt will break toward. The lower you can crouch behind the ball, the better you'll be able to read any breaks. That's why, if a green is elevated, you'll often see players walk down the slope to study the putt from ground level.

Like a number of players, I like to plumb-bob my putts. I stand several feet behind my ball, on a flat part of the green if possible.

The Putting Stroke. I putt from a slightly open stance, with the ball positioned off my left heel. This stance helps me see the line of my putt more easily. My eyes are inside the target line. Unlike some players who "jab" their putts, I concentrate on making a smooth stroke and accelerating through the ball.

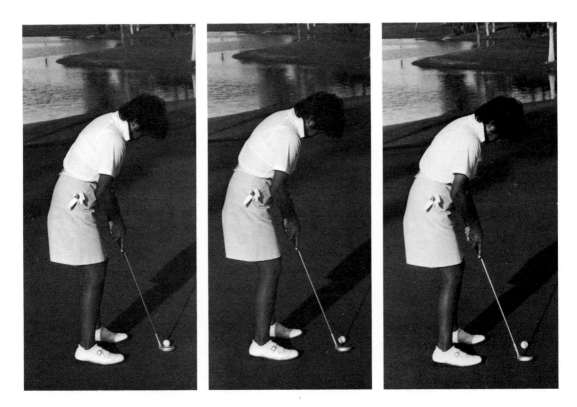

This is the same putting stroke viewed from both sides. Mine is a very long, unhurried stroke—smooth, controlled by the big muscles of my

arms and shoulders, with very little wrist break.

Holding the putter between my thumb and forefinger, I let it hang down in front of my face, so the shaft covers a line between the ball and the hole. I close one eye, just as if I were sighting a gun. If there is any space between the ball and the hole, the space is the amount the putt will break. I use plumb-bobbing as a way to reinforce my initial read of the putt.

My general rule is that first impressions are the best impressions. I don't think looking at a putt from behind the hole or from above the hole is particularly helpful. In fact, I think you run the risk of overreading a putt and confusing yourself. Your brain can only absorb so much information before chaos sets in up there.

It is important to take the grain of the grass into account, particularly if you are playing on Bermuda grass greens, which are especially grainy.

There are two good ways to read the grain. First, if you study the putt, and the grass seems shiny, the grain is away from you. If the grass looks dull and dark, the grain is toward you, and the putt will be slower. Second, you can study the grass around the cup. For example, if the grain is east to west, the grass right on the east edge of the cup will look normal, but the grass on the west side will be sparse, because the grass was cut off at the base when the hole was cut.

Keep in mind that the grain will have a greater effect later in the day as the grass gets longer. The grain will also tend toward the west, or the setting sun. And last but not least, the grain will have a greater effect on a slowly hit putt than it will on a firm putt. That's why, quite often, you'll see players hit short putts very firmly: they are taking the grain, and often the break, right out of play altogether and slam-dunking the ball into the cup.

The Last Step

Once I've read the putt, I pick an intermediate target to aim at, just as I do for my full shots. I look for an odd-colored blade of grass or an old pitch mark on the line of the putt, a foot or so from my ball. Then I walk into the putt, carefully setting the putter down behind the ball so that the blade is square with the target line. My putter must not move as I address the putt. First I carefully put my right hand on the grip, with the palm parallel to the putterface and square with the target line. Then I put my left hand on the club and finish building my stance. Again, as I'm addressing the ball, my focus is on my intermediate target.

Once I've taken my stance, my focus shifts to the hole, and I'll take a couple of practice strokes to get a feel for the distance of the putt and how hard I have to hit the ball. Once I've done that, my focus shifts back to my intermediate target one last time, just to make sure my putter is aligned properly. Then I pull the trigger.

That last point is very important when it comes to putts that have a lot of break. Too often I see players—even some very good players—steal one last glance at the hole. That sends a mixed signal to your brain. Again, once you've picked an intermediate target, that should be the last target you check before you putt. Start it out over that spot, and with the right speed and a little luck you'll get your long putts closer to the hole, and more of your short and medium-length putts into the hole, than you ever thought possible.

CHIPPING
Part Golf Shot, Part Putt

First of all, let me clear up some confusion. People often mix up chipping and pitching. Here's how I've always described the difference: A chip is a shot that flies a short distance in the air and then runs a longer distance along the green. A pitch is usually a higher shot and one that carries farther in the air than it runs along the green.

A chip is usually played from the fringe, or collar, of the green, when there's too much of the longer grass to comfortably try to putt the ball over. There's an old saying in golf that "a bad putt will usually be better than a good chip." I think there's a lot of truth to that. When you are putting, you have only two considerations: the speed of the putt and the line. When you chip the ball, you have to factor in how far you want to fly the ball and how much spin it may have when it lands. Again, my first rule in golf is to keep life as simple as possible, so if I have a choice between chipping the ball and putting it, I'll putt it 99 percent of the time.

Still, there are times when chipping the ball is the smart play. As I said, you may have a lot of fringe to carry, or you may have a long distance to the hole, and a chip may be easier to control than trying to hit a putter especially hard.

Learning to become a good chipper isn't really as difficult as many people make it seem, but it does require understanding certain fundamentals—and, of course, experience and practice.

Club Selection

There are two schools of thought on picking the right club to chip with, and I fall somewhere in between the two.

The first school argues that you should find one club that you are comfortable with and hit the majority of your chips with that club, varying the distance by opening or closing the clubface or by hitting the shot harder or softer.

While I don't entirely agree with that thinking, there is some merit to using a club you have confidence in. I hit many of my chips with an 8-iron. If I need to, I can hood the club slightly, turning it into a club with the loft of a 7-iron or even a 6-iron if I need the ball to run. Or, if I want the ball to check up, I can open the blade and cut across the ball slightly, in effect making my 8-iron play like a 9-iron or even a pitching wedge. This is an example of how my feel and experience come into play with my shotmaking.

The second school also has a good point, particularly for the weekend player. Proponents of this approach argue that it's a lot easier to keep the same basic chipping swing but to change clubs according to each situation. For example, where I might finesse an 8-iron into a pitching wedge shot, they would simply take the pitching wedge and play a straightforward shot. As I say, that point of view has a lot of merit, particularly among newer golfers. Too often, I see players trying to hit chips with their "favorite club" that the most gifted shotmaker in history couldn't pull off.

I should point out that there are an awful lot of very good chippers who teach that you should never use less than a 7-iron to chip with. They suggest using mid-irons, since these clubs will put very little spin on the ball. Their point—and it's a good one—is that by virtually eliminating spin as a consideration, you've made the shot just one step easier to plan and pull off.

Either way, I think you've got to experiment and practice to see which approach is going to work best for you. Now let's spend a minute on the mechanics of the chip shot.

Preshot Routine

Since the chip is essentially a putt, you should study the shot just as you would a putt. Look for the break and the speed of the green. Now here's the difference between a chip and other shots: you want to pick both an intermediate target for aiming and a spot where you want the ball to land and begin rolling toward the hole.

Only experience can teach you how far a ball should carry in the air and how far it will roll with any given shot. The key is, once you've picked where you want the ball to land, visualize the shot and the ball landing on that spot and rolling smoothly toward the hole. Just as with the long, breaking putts, your target is the spot where you want the ball to land, not the hole itself.

Stance

A chip is basically a hands-and-arms swing. There is very little movement of either your upper or lower body. I like to open my stance slightly, pulling my left foot back off the target line. My feet

Chipping the Ball. Making solid contact is the key to good chipping. To do this, I play the ball back in my stance and hit the ball with a descending blow. My hands are ahead of the ball at impact. I like to play from a slightly open stance. There's very little body movement with a chip shot. It's basically an arm stroke.

Chipping the Ball (side view). There are two keys to good chipping, and these photographs illustrate them very well. First, unless you have to carry the ball a fair distance, there is very little wrist break in a chip shot. It is basically an arm stroke. The length of the swing determines how far the ball will fly, but try to avoid decelerating the clubhead at

impact. If you have a short chip, make a short backswing. Second, notice that the clubhead stays pretty much on a straight path. It moves slightly inside the line, but I like to think of it as a mini-takeaway—a copy of the first few feet of my regular swing.

The 8-Iron Chip. Occasionally you'll find yourself in this spot. The ball is sitting down in the rough bordering the green. Rather than using a wedge, take your 8-iron, open your stance, set your hands ahead of the ball, and pinch down on the ball with a descending blow. The ball will pop out and settle softly.

8-Iron Chip (side view). Too often I see my amateur partners fall into the trap of hitting all their chips with the same club. That forces them to make a different swing for every shot. Here's an example where I'm better off using an 8-iron. The ball is sitting up nicely in the rough, so all I want to do is get the ball over the fringe and rolling smoothly toward the hole. I grip down on the club for better control, open my stance,

and keep my knees flexed throughout the shot. I take the club back in one piece with my arms and shoulders. There's very little wrist cock. Then I sweep it off the grass, unlike a normal pitch where I hit down on the ball. Notice that the clubface remains aimed at the target throughout the follow-through. I want to avoid putting any side spin on the ball.

are fairly close together, perhaps a foot or so apart, and my weight is set mostly on my left side.

I address the ball with my hands ahead of the ball, which is set back slightly in my stance. I also position the ball closer to my body than I do for full shots. These fundamentals allow me to hit down on the ball. I also grip down on the club, since this gives me a better sense of feel and control.

Unless I have to carry the ball a fairly good distance, I try to avoid cocking my wrists very much, if at all. I simply take the club back straight away from the ball and sweep down and through. There isn't much of a follow-through. I'm just interested in making solid contact every time. If I can do that, I won't have many surprises. Players who don't make solid contact with their chip shots are in for a surprise every time they hit a shot. I think golf has enough surprises without dealing with the ones I can prevent.

THE PITCH SHOT
More Air Time, Less Ground Time

The pitch is a valuable shot in a number of areas. First, it's a good shot to know if you have to land the ball softly, trying to get to a pin placement when you don't have a lot of green to work with. It's also the basic shot for hitting the ball out of the rough that usually surrounds the green.

Once you learn the basics of pitching the ball, you can experiment, creating all sorts of shots around the green that will help you get the ball up and down to save par.

Club Selection

Unlike a chip shot, when you have the choice of a variety of clubs, for all intents and purposes pitch shots are hit with either a pitching wedge or a sand wedge.

The advantage of a sand wedge is that it has more loft than a pitching wedge, and this makes it easier to get the ball up in the air quickly and impart more spin to the ball than a pitching wedge. If you are planning to use your sand wedge as a pitching club, make sure that it doesn't have an excessive amount of bounce. The more bounce a club has, the higher the leading edge of the club will sit above the ground when you lay the blade open. The higher the leading edge sits above the turf, the greater your chances of blading the ball.

There are a few solutions to this problem. You can take your sand wedge to a professional and have some of the bounce ground off the club. Be aware, however, that the less bounce a club has, the less effective it can be in the bunkers, especially in bunkers with fine, deep sand. You can also invest in a specialty wedge or a 60-degree wedge. This club is designed specifically for hitting high, soft pitch shots. I'd recommend this club if you play at a course that demands this kind of shot frequently in a round. The last solution is to become more versatile with your pitching wedge. It has almost no bounce, so you can open the blade without fear of blading the ball.

I like to play most of my pitch shots with my sand wedge, because it doesn't have nearly as much bounce as the wedges you'll find in most golf shops. I can use this club because I've practiced my bunker play a great deal, so my sand wedge is an extremely versatile club.

Pitching the Ball. The pitch shot is a mini full swing. I play from a narrow, slightly open stance. The length of my shot determines the length of my swing, but the key is to accelerate through the swing. Too often, players take a backswing that is too long, and decelerate at impact, usually with horrible results.

The pitch shot from the side view—note how the backswing and follow-through are fuller than for the chip shot. That means there are more variables to learn to control through practice of this versatile shot.

Stance

My stance is a little wider than my chipping stance, because a pitch requires a longer swing, and my stance has to be wide enough to support that swing. I open my stance slightly, pulling my left foot back off the target line. This gets my left leg and hip out of the way, which is particularly important if I try to cut across the ball from outside the line, trying to put increased spin on the ball.

Ball Position

You want to position the ball forward in your stance. Begin with it off your left heel and then experiment, moving it forward in your stance as you become more comfortable with the shot. Within reason, the farther you move the ball forward in your stance, the higher and softer you'll be able to hit your pitch shots.

Hand Position and Grip

The secret to hitting good pitch shots is in your hands. You want to set your hands even with, or even slightly behind, the ball at address. The mistake I see a lot of golfers make is setting their hands ahead of the ball at address, then pinching down on the ball at impact. In effect, they've turned their wedges into 9-irons or, in extreme cases, 8-irons. That explains why they can't hit the high, soft pitch they had in mind.

You also need a nice, light grip pressure for these shots. You want to make a wristy release at impact, sliding the clubhead under the ball to put a lot of spin on the ball, which will help the ball stop more quickly once it lands.

The Swing

A pitch shot is largely an arm-and-shoulder swing. Your feet stay planted on the ground; there's virtually no hip turn unless you get a fair distance from the target. The distance you hit the ball is controlled by the length of the swing. You want to guard against making a long backswing, only to decelerate coming into the ball. Also, keep in mind that the more you swing on an outside-to-inside swing path—cutting the ball—the higher the shot will fly, but what you gain in height you will lose in distance.

As I said earlier, the pitch shot can be one of the most versatile shots in your bag. But it will take practice to learn how to control the variables: length of swing, open clubface, ball and hand positions, swing path.

LAST MINUTE HELP
Play like a Child

Kids are great students in golf because they trust their instincts and don't get bogged down by all the stuff they've heard before. That should be a good lesson for all of us. Whenever possible, think like a child and trust your instincts.

In this chapter we talked about picking a target to land your

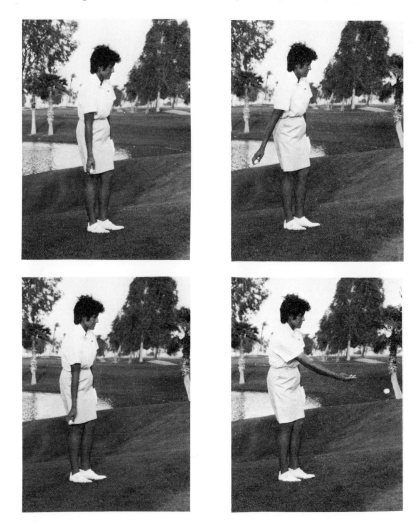

My Playground Drill. Some people have a hard time chipping and pitching the ball because they have difficulty visualizing how far the ball should carry in the air and how far it should roll. If you have that problem, take a ball and pitch it toward the hole. After a few tries you'll have a feel for how you have to throw the ball to get it close to the hole. Once you do, try to duplicate the ball flight with your pitch and chip shots.

chips and pitches and then letting them run to the hole. If that's confusing or you're having a tough time putting the idea into action, try this instead:

Take a handful of golf balls and go stand by a green. Now check the distance to the pin and decide how you'd have to throw the ball underhanded to get it to stop near the hole. If you have a short distance, you'll instinctively—I hope—either throw the ball a little higher or a little softer. If you have a greater distance, you'll either throw a little lower or higher but harder.

Try this drill, and I think it will open your eyes to the many possibilities you have around the greens—and the many little shots you have that can help you save big numbers on your scorecard.

Lopez File: Kathy Whitworth

Kathy Whitworth is a player I admire very much. It's hard to say that a player who has won 88 professional tour events is underrated, but I honestly think Kathy has never received the recognition she deserves.

I'm not big on going to other players for advice, but Kathy is someone I admire so much that I will ask her for her help.

We've talked in this book about how important a good short game is, and Kathy is living proof. She is a player who can get it up and down from a trash can, and that ability has won a lot of tournaments for her. I rank her with JoAnne Carner, Sandra Haynie, and Sandra Palmer as probably being the most knowledgeable players on the LPGA tour when it comes to the swing and shotmaking.

Obviously, Kathy is a very good competitor. Nobody backs into that many tournament wins. She has a very strong, but very quiet, personality. I remember when I first played with her I was surprised how she'd talk to herself during a round.

"C'mon, Kathy," she'd say, "Why'd you do a dumb thing like that?"

For a while, I thought this was the sign of a negative attitude, but I learned that it is just Kathy's way of motivating herself to play better.

When I watch her play, I don't see the outward signs of competitiveness I see with JoAnne or Amy. She just goes out there and plays her game, trying as hard as she can on every shot.

Kathy came out on tour in 1958, at a time when there were a number of good players, but the tour didn't have the depth it has today. People sometimes ask how I think she would have done if she had come out when Amy, Hollis, Jan, and I did. I tell them that players like Kathy—true champions—will find a way to win. That's why it's impossible to compare players from one era with those of another. The one thing champions all have in common is a great deal of pride—in themselves, in their game, in their record.

Not everyone can have Kathy Whitworth's skill. Not everyone can have her short game. But everyone, no matter what his or her handicap, can have her pride. She wants to win every time she tees up. But every bit as important, she wants to do herself proud by trying her hardest on every shot.

And she does.

5

Bunker Shots: End Your Fear of Sand Forever

I'm going to tell you something right now that 90 percent of you won't believe: the basic, straightforward, everyday, run-of-the-mill sand shot is one of the easiest shots in golf.

Why? Because in almost every other shot the clubhead makes contact with the ball, and the more precise that contact, the better the shot. In the bunker, it's the sand that throws the ball out. All the clubhead does is displace the sand.

Look at it this way: suppose you put a tennis ball in a swimming pool, then set your hand open to about the same degree of loft as a sand wedge. Now, if you drove your hand down into the water and kept it going under the ball, the water your hand displaces would throw the ball out. A sand wedge works the same way as your hand. On top of that, you've got a wide choice of clubs designed to glide through the sand and get the ball out.

Why do people panic in bunkers? First of all, a bunker is defined a hazard by the rules, and anything that's called a hazard must be hazardous, right? It might surprise you to learn that there are times when, faced with all the options, I'll deliberately try to hit the ball at the bunker, because that leaves me a safer and easier shot to the pin than I might have from the deep rough. That's why, if you watch a tournament on television, you might hear a player say, "Get in the bunker," if a shot is off line. That golfer is playing the percentages.

THE BASIC SAND SHOT

Let's run through the fundamentals of playing a bunker shot and see if we can do something to improve your percentage of success the next time you find yourself in the sand.

Equipment

The most important fundamental is a good sand club. We've covered this earlier, but I want to stress again that a good sand wedge can make or break you in the bunkers. If you are an average-handicap player or higher, you want to make sure your wedge has plenty of bounce, since this is what allows the clubhead to glide through the sand without digging in the way a pitching wedge will. Bounce is particularly important if you play in places where the sand is very soft and fine.

Better players can experiment with wedges with less bounce and a narrow, more rounded flange. This design not only lets them use their sand wedge as a pitching club, but also lets them hit more precise sand shots.

Here's a tip for better players: you might consider changing the shaft in your sand club. A number of players like a softer or more flexible shaft in their sand clubs, since this lets the shaft do more of the work. Still others like a firm shaft, because they want more control. Experiment to see which shaft works best for you. You might also try a shaft that's an inch or so longer, since this will help when you find yourself in awkward lies with the ball well below your feet.

There's also a lot of discussion among better players about how heavy a sand wedge should be. Some players prefer a wedge that's lighter than the rest of their irons, since they believe this improves their touch. Other players prefer a heavier sand wedge, because the extra head weight helps in buried lies or in playing from the rough. Still others want all their irons to feel the same, and they adjust their wedges accordingly. I suggest experimenting to see which feels best for you.

Stance

The sand shot is played from an open stance, since this allows you to slide the clubhead easily under the ball. The mistake people often make is that they set the club behind the ball, then open the clubface,

Set your feet—working your feet into the sand will give you more stability and will also give you a feel for the texture of the sand.

then open the stance. This is wrong in about three different ways. Let me give you a routine that will work for you:

1. Open the clubface. Remember, the more you open the clubface, the higher—and shorter—the ball will fly.

2. Aim the clubface at your target. Remember to take into account any break on the green.

3. Grip the club. The idea is to have the clubface set open to the proper degree before you grip the club. Gripping the club and then turning your hands to open the clubface practically guarantees you'll close down the clubface at impact.

4. Take your stance. Work your feet into the ground an inch or so. This will give you a feel for how firm the sand is, it will give you a solid base to play from, and it will automatically lower your swing arc so that, instead of making contact with the ball, you will slide the clubhead an inch or so underneath it—but only if you trust your swing. Remember, you want to play from an open stance so that, if lines were drawn across you feet, knees, and shoulders, they would all point to a spot left of the target.

To hit this shot best, think about swinging along your body lines. By that I mean take the club back outside the target line, then trust

Playing from the Sand. To hit a bunker shot, I open my stance and open the blade of my sand wedge. I aim to the left of my intended target, and then swing along the line of my body, taking the club back outside the target line and cutting under the ball, accelerating to a nice, full finish.

Out of the sand viewed from the side. A smooth, accelerating swing is better than a big, full swing.

your swing to slide the clubhead under the ball. Keep accelerating the clubhead through the sand, swinging toward a point left of the target. Since the clubface is open, it will direct the sand—and the ball—toward your target.

You don't need a big, full swing for this shot. It's better just to have nice, smooth swing that accelerates the clubhead through the sand. Resist the temptation to stop at the ball and look up to see where it went. If you do that, most of the time you won't have to look very far. The ball will still be in the sand with you.

SOME SPECIALTY SHOTS

Once you master the basic sand shot, there are some other shots that might help you save strokes in the bunker. The key to these shots is keeping your wits about you and concentrating on the fundamentals.

Pitching the Ball

If you have a good lie and a bunker with very little lip, sometimes the smart play is simply to pitch—or even chip—the ball out and let it run to the hole. Play the shot just as we discussed in the previous chapter. You'll want to square your stance and the clubface and play the ball slightly back in your stance. Since both your stance and the clubface are square, you'll want to take dead aim on your target. The key to this shot is making solid contact, which is why you move the ball back in your stance and set your hands ahead—then just punch down on the ball. Depending on how far you have to hit this shot, you might experiment with a pitching wedge, 9-iron, or 8-iron.

Remember, this shot won't work if you have anything less than a perfect lie or if you have much of a lip. But it is a safe shot and a little less wearing on your nerves if you don't quite yet have confidence in playing an explosion shot from the sand.

Stopping the Ball

There are two ways to stop a shot. Either it comes in very high, or it comes in with spin. In most bunker shots, you can't get enough height, so you must have spin.

Unless you have perfect conditions—a good lie, a green that is either flat or sloping toward you, and a green that isn't too firm—you should forget this shot. Take your medicine and play for two putts.

To put spin on the ball, you must slip the clubface very close to the ball. The less sand you take, the more spin you can impart. Obviously, the closer you come to the ball, the greater the chance for a mistake. That makes this a very difficult shot to hit with a club that's loaded with bounce.

You set up to the ball the same way you would for a normal sand shot, but you cock your wrists sharply on the backswing. Then you must try to slip the clubface under the ball with a flicking motion, coming as close to the ball as you can and finishing very high.

I have to stress that this is a risky shot. You have to know what you're doing, when you need to do it, and whether your nerves will let you try.

The Buried Lie. Occasionally you'll face a shot where the ball is partially buried in the sand. Don't panic. Play the ball back in your stance. Close your stance and square the clubface.

Drive the clubface under the ball, keeping your left wrist firm at impact. There won't be much follow-through, and allow for plenty of roll because the ball won't check like a regular bunker shot.

The Buried Lie

When a ball comes into a bunker very high, or when the sand is soft, you run the risk of having the ball bury itself in the sand. There's no need to panic; just make a couple of adjustments.

To hit this shot, particularly if the ball is buried deeply, you just want to drive the clubhead into the sand and gouge the ball out. It isn't going to be pretty. If you try to slide the clubhead under the ball, you run an excellent risk of blading the ball into worse shape.

You'll want to close your stance and square up your clubface. You want the clubhead to dig into the sand behind the ball. It's almost like a punch shot. There's no follow-through.

Keep in mind that the ball is going to come out low and hot, so allow for plenty of roll. This is not a shot to get cute with and turn a one-shot mistake into the quickest triple bogey you've ever seen.

You'll have to practice and experiment to see what you can get away with. If the ball is just slightly buried, you can still play a variation of your regular sand shot. As the lie becomes worse, you have to change your shot and lower your expectations.

One final thought: some players, when faced with a badly buried ball, will forget a sand wedge altogether and use a pitching wedge, since it's an easier club to drive into the sand. It might be worth a few minutes of experimenting to see if it will work for you.

When the ball comes into the bunker from on high, or when the sand is soft, a buried lie is what you get.

FAIRWAY BUNKERS
Play the Percentages

The first and most important rule when you find yourself in a fairway bunker is "Get the ball out." Too often people try to be heroes by playing for the green, only to leave the ball in the sand or, worse, plugged up under the lip.

As you study the shot, make two decisions: (1) How much club do I need to carry the lip of the bunker? (2) If I can hit enough club to reach the green, where's the safest place to play to?

Once you've made your club selection, set up to the ball with a square or slightly open stance and work your feet into the sand, You want to get a feel for the sand and anchor yourself, but since you want to pick the ball off the sand, make sure you grip down on the club the same amount that you buried your feet in the sand. If you don't do this, you run the risk of hitting the shot fat and leaving it in the bunker.

The important thing in a fairway bunker is ensuring that you hit first the ball and then the sand. You give yourself a larger margin for error if you try to hit the shot thin rather than fat.

You don't want to hurry the shot. Make your normal swing and try to concentrate on nipping the ball cleanly. This is one shot where you want to pick the ball off the sand, rather than hit the ball with a descending blow as you do with most other shots.

I suggest you hit these shots with irons rather than woods. With a wood, you run the risk of the club bouncing off the sand and topping the ball. I think an iron is easier to control under the circumstances. Plus, your woods will last a lot longer if you're not sandblasting them all the time.

Fairway Bunker Shots. The first consideration is to take enough club to get the ball over the front lip of the bunker. Once you've picked the club, address the ball with a slightly open stance, and make sure you work your feet into the sand to give you added support. The key to this shot is hitting the ball cleanly. Remember: Ball first, sand second.

The fairway bunker viewed
from the side—pick the ball
off the sand, rather than hit
the ball a descending blow.

Lopez File: Julie Inkster

Photo courtesy of Robert Walker.

Just a quick look at Julie's record tells you how good a player she really is. She won three U.S. Amateurs, played on a Curtis Cup team and two World Cup teams, and has won eight times since coming out on tour in 1983. Last year she won four times and finished third on the money list with almost $300,000 in winnings.

Julie is really a good ball striker, and I think she's one of the most complete players on tour. It's hard to point to a weakness in her game, but I think one of her real strengths is that she plays with what she's got. She rarely tries anything she thinks she might not be able to pull off. As a result, you rarely see her play defensive golf.

Obviously, when you look at somebody who has won as often as Julie, you know she has to be a good competitor, and I see it the most when she hits a shot she's not thrilled with. That's when the sparks sometimes fly. I'm not talking about a temper tantrum, but you can tell that she expects a lot from herself and her game, and she isn't happy with anything less than the best.

Oftentimes people who display a little temper get criticized, but within reason—and Julie is well within reason—it's just their competitiveness coming through. I just think you need to have that kind of pride to become really good in anything, but especially in something as demanding as golf.

Besides all her natural ability and competitiveness, one thing I really admire in Julie is her ability to be her own person. She's able to keep her career and her life in balance, and that helps keep her centered. Too often, I see players on our tour who just live for their golf, and when they start playing badly it consumes them because golf is all they have in their lives. These are the players who get in world-class slumps or who burn out very early.

I think Julie is going to be a very good player for a long time, just for that reason. She knows that golf is only one part of her life, and while it's important, it isn't the be-all and end-all that it is for other players.

If there's one thing all of us can learn from watching Julie Inkster, it's how well she goes with the flow on the course. If she hits a bad shot or gets a bad break, she blows off a little steam and then gets back to the job at hand.

Now I'm not saying that everyone should go out and start tossing clubs into trees after a bad swing. But too often I see players let bad shots or tough breaks bother them, and the result is a series of bad shots, more anger and frustration, and finally a meltdown as the round falls totally apart. You'll never see that happen to a player like Julie Inkster.

6

Developing Distance: How to Hit It Farther

Everybody wants to hit the ball farther. I do. You do. It's just human nature. It also makes this game a lot easier if you are hitting middle irons into greens while your opponents are trying to get home with long irons or fairway woods.

There's a price you have to pay for distance, and that's accuracy. It doesn't do you any good to be 15 or 20 yards longer than everyone off the tee, if they're playing their second shots from the fairway and you're playing yours from out in the jungle.

Golf isn't a game of inches. In truth, it's a game of fractions of inches, which turn into yards. Let me explain. If I hit a tee shot 220 yards with my clubface one degree open at impact, the ball will probably still be in the fairway. At worst, it will be in the first cut of rough.

Now, let's say I really rip into a drive and hit it 250 yards with the clubface again open one degree at impact. Now I'm looking at a shot from the deep rough, and I've negated whatever advantage I had from a drive that was 30 yards longer—in reality, hitting either two or three clubs less into the green.

So my first rule is "distance without direction is worse than no distance at all."

The key to having both distance and direction is making solid

Driving for Distance. When I want to really let out the shaft and try for extra yards, I try to draw the ball from right to left. To do that, I set up with a slightly closed stance. I take the club away low and slow. I don't want to get fast with my swing.

I make a full turn on my backswing, coiling the muscles in my upper body and shoulders. I drive through the ball, extending fully as my hands release at impact. Timing is the key to power. Clubhead speed that is out of control spells nothing but trouble.

contact every time, and that's pretty hard to do if you are swinging out of your shoes, trying to murder the ball.

Most really good players swing at about 75 percent of full speed. That is a swing they can control but that will still deliver enough clubhead speed to hit a good drive. When they need a bigger drive, they increase their swing speed slightly, but never more than 90 percent, because anything faster than that is a swing headed out of control. No matter how hard a good player is trying to hit a shot, he or she will always be in balance at the finish of the swing. How many high handicappers can you say that about?

I'm fortunate in that my swing is so slow and rhythmic that it's unusual for me to get into a rut of swinging too hard. When I do, I know that I have a tendency to jump at the ball once I've finished my backswing. The results are usually pretty pathetic.

When I do need a little more yardage, I concentrate on maintaining a good tempo throughout the swing. My last thought before beginning my swing is "Low and slow." I want to get good extension away from the ball so that the clubhead will move in the widest possible arc.

I focus very hard on the ball, because this helps me make solid contact. Very often, I see players actually close their eyes prior to impact, which must be some kind of instinctive reaction. The problem is, this deprives your brain of a vital piece of information—where the ball is. Again, the old saying "Keep your eye on the ball" really is true when it comes to golf.

It's important that you finish the swing, driving through impact to a nice high finish. A lot of times you'll see players who are in such a hurry to follow the ball that they forget to finish their swing. What they usually see is their ball heading for the woods on the right.

Earlier we talked about hitting a draw. If you are trying to add a few yards, a shot that flies from right to left is the shot you should play, since it has overspin and will run farther than a fade or even a straight shot. In that section, I suggested trying to make contact right on the back-left quarter of the ball, since this will help you make an inside-to-down-the-line swing path. There's also another benefit to this: it will help prevent you from coming over the top.

Coming over the top simply means that instead of the clubhead coming into the ball from either the inside or down the line, it comes from outside the line. This results in either a big slice, as the

Teeing the Ball. People are often confused about how high to tee the ball. I like to tee it just high enough so that the center, or equator, of the ball is aligned with the top of my driver.

clubhead cuts across the ball, or a shot that's pulled to the left. Either way, it spells trouble.

Coming over the top on a shot is often caused by the desire to "hit at" the ball rather than "swing through" the ball. That's why I like to tell people just to let the ball get in the way of the clubhead as they swing. That tendency to hit at the ball is one reason most people have practice swings that look better than their regular swings. Without a ball to worry about, they can make a nice, smooth pass. Put a ball down, and suddenly lights and buzzers go off in their brain, and they become ball-bound.

Here's a drill that will help you develop both distance and direction:

Go to the practice tee and, once you've warmed up, take out your driver. The trick is to try to make a good, full swing but at a speed you think will let you make solid contact and hit the ball 100 yards. If 100 yards is your best drive to begin with, then try to hit the ball 50 yards. Whatever the distance, I want you to feel that you are swinging at about 50 percent of full speed.

The point is, I want you thinking about making solid contact with a nice, smooth swing. I don't want you thinking about driving for distance just yet.

Driving for distance viewed from the side.
Timing, not speed, is the key to power.

Once you've succeeded in hitting several solid shots, I hope you'll see how much farther the ball is carrying than you had planned. Now it's time to crank up your swing a little bit. If you were at 50 percent, move up to 60 percent, and stay there until you hit several balls in a row solidly. Remember, even though you are swinging slightly harder, keep all the parts of your swing working together. Don't let any one part—your hands, legs, arms, whatever—get out of control, because one part can throw the whole swing out of whack.

Keep doing this drill until you feel you are swinging at 75–80 percent of full swing. With any luck, you won't have to swing any harder than that, because you should be swinging at a pace that will give you all the length you need.

One final thought about developing distance. There's a tendency in golf to overdo things. We are all guilty of finding something that works and then exaggerating it until it doesn't work anymore.

Tom Kite, who is a player I like and admire very much, has a saying he learned from Harvey Pennick, the professional who taught him to play as a boy. Mr. Pennick told Tom, "An aspirin will probably cure what ails you, but the whole bottle will almost certainly kill you."

That's pretty good advice when it comes to golf. And almost everything else.

Lopez File: Hollis Stacy

Photo courtesy of Robert Walker.

Hollis and I go way back. Beginning in 1969, she won three straight U.S. Junior Girls' Championships. That seemed like such a good idea that I came along in 1972 and did the same thing.

Hollis has an outstanding record, with 17 tour victories since turning pro in 1974. In fact, from 1977 until 1986 she managed to win at least one tournament a year.

Still, Hollis's greatest accomplishment may be that she's won three U.S. Women's Opens, including back-to-back Opens in 1977 and 1978. The Open is probably the toughest tournament we play. For starters, the USGA holds the championship on some of the best courses in the country, and they are set up very hard. Lots of rough. Tough pin placements. Fast greens.

On top of all that, the pressure is greater at the Open than at any other tournament, especially for the good players. I know that it's the one tournament I really want to win, since it's the only major I haven't won yet. In the past, that pressure has made me try too hard, and it's cost me a few good chances to win.

There are a lot of players who see the USGA flag go up and fall apart. They might as well go home. Hollis is just the opposite. She thrives on the pressure of the Open, perhaps because her mom, Tillie, has been a USGA committee member for a long time.

Hollis is a strong competitor—when she wants to play. Just the fact she's 6–1 in playoffs tells you how tough she is. It's funny, though, if she decides she doesn't want any part of the competition, there's no one more laid-back. Of all the really good players I know, I think Hollis is the most hot and cold about the game.

I think that, by and large, Hollis just doesn't have the motivation she once did. That's easy enough to understand, since she's been playing very good golf for a very long time. She's 33 now, and I think she's looking around to see what else life has to offer beyond golf and the tour.

When Hollis wants to play, there's nobody like her around the greens. She's got a fabulous touch and lots of imagination, which is what all the players with good short games have in common. She can visualize shots that other people can't even imagine. As for her putting, only Betsy King comes close to being as good as Hollis.

One reason Hollis's short game is so good is that she's tested it in competition for all these years. Chances are, you won't have the chance to do that, but here's something that might work for you: If you are out playing by yourself, and the course isn't crowded, play two or three approach shots to the greens. No matter where those balls end up, play out the hole with each of them. I think this is a better way to practice than just hitting a lot of pitch shots to a practice green, because the conditions are a lot more realistic. The key is concentrating very hard on each shot, just as though you were in competition. That way, when you need to hit these shots under the gun, you'll have the imagination to be able to visualize them and the experience to be able to pull them off.

7

How to Practice: The Key to Improving

There has never been a good player who didn't practice, although different players practice differently. Some very technical or mechanical players love to spend long hours on the practice tee or green, breaking down their game and analyzing it. For more natural players, like me, it's a place to go to find what's right or wrong, work out the kinks, and move on to something else.

Whatever type of player you are, here are some guidelines that will help you make more effective use of your practice time.

Stretch for Success. The golf swing can put a lot of strain on your body, especially your lower back. This stretching exercise is one I do to prevent injuries. Just put a club behind your shoulders and turn slowly from side to side. It's also a good way to get the feel for a proper turn.

WARMING UP
Giving Yourself a Chance

For starters, the time to practice is after your round. I've seen a lot of players who hit so many balls prior to a round that they leave their game on the practice tee. They simply don't have enough strength left to finish a round.

That's not to say that you should scrimp on the time you have for warming up. I've never understood players who race to the first tee, take a couple of practice swings, and expect to have a good round. It will take them a good three holes to warm up, and by that time they've hit so many bizarre shots that they are confused, frustrated, or just too mad to think straight. On top of that, they stand a good chance of hurting their backs because they haven't stretched and loosened their muscles.

I like to arrive at the course early enough to have plenty of time to warm up, but not so early that I have to stand around and kill time, waiting to tee off. Before I leave for the course, I make it a point to do about 10 minutes worth of stretching, to loosen up my back, legs, arms, and shoulders. If I don't stretch, I feel tight and run the risk of getting one of those nagging injuries that seem to take forever to go away.

When I get to the practice tee, I begin hitting a few soft wedge shots, just to develop some feel and establish a nice, slow tempo. Once I've done that, I begin to work my way through my bag, skipping every other club. I'll go to a 9-iron, a 7-iron, a 5-iron, and so forth. I always make sure that the last shot I hit with any club is a good one. I don't want any doubts entering my mind the first time I pull the club out of the bag on the course.

I also make it a point to find a swing or key that seems to be working for me. As I've said, my basic thought is to take the club away from the ball low and slow on my backswing, but occasionally I'll work on another thought if "low and slow" isn't working quite well enough. As Bobby Jones once said when someone asked him what his favorite swing thought was: "Whichever one worked best last."

I'll also work especially hard on specific shots I need to hit during the round. I remember playing in Hawaii one year, and it was so windy that we had to hit 2-irons and 3-irons into a lot of the par fours. I made it a point to hit a lot of those before my round.

Before I leave the practice tee I make sure I hit a few shots like the one I'll face on the first tee. If that drive calls for a fade, then I'll hit a few fades with my driver to get my swing ready and establish my confidence and a good mental image. After I've done that, I'll hit a few more soft wedges to gear down and sharpen my sense of feel.

In the time remaining, I'll go to the practice green and hit some chips and putts, again, mostly just to work on my feel. I'm mostly concerned with getting a feel for distance when I'm hitting putts. As I said before, more people three-putt because they had the wrong distance than because they had the wrong line.

AFTER THE ROUND
Now the Work Really Begins

I doubt that there's ever been anyone who practiced more than Ben Hogan, but he had a secret. He would have only 25 or so balls in his practice bag. After he hit those, he would take a break and wait while his caddie brought the balls back to the tee. Mr. Hogan said he carried only 25 balls because if he carried more he'd hit them too fast, wind up hitting too many, and not have time to think about what he was working on.

There are at least two good lessons we can all learn from that story. First of all, you should never practice without a thought in mind. Work on one part of your swing—maybe two at the most—in any practice session. Once you've worked out the problem, take the day off. It's also a good idea to keep a little notebook in your bag and jot down what you worked on and what the solution was. You'll be surprised by how often the same problems recur in the swing.

The other lesson was to take your time. I watch people fire out practice balls like a machine gun and then complain because they aren't improving. Of course they aren't. They don't have time to think about what they are doing—and what they are really doing is ingraining a whole lot of bad habits into their swing.

I know there are a lot of people who just find practicing boring. If you're one of them, maybe this will help. Instead of just hitting balls, make believe every ball represents a shot during a round. Actually visualize the course conditions—where the pin is cut, where the bunkers are, how the match stands. Make it as realistic as possible, to the point of going through your preshot routine on every shot. I even know some players who play an entire round during a practice session. They begin with the drive on the first hole and end up with their approach to 18. All that's missing is the putting—and for all I know, they head over to the practice green and do that, too. This not only helps their shotmaking but does wonders for their concentration as well.

It's a good idea to find someone who knows your swing. In my case it has always been my father, although Ray, because he has an athlete's eye, is also getting pretty good at spotting what I'm doing wrong. In your case, it will probably be a professional. Try to avoid taking advice from your friends. They are trying to be helpful, but

I'm afraid that in most cases they will be trying to shape your swing either to a model that doesn't fit your body or to the latest theory they read in a golf magazine. Either way, you lose.

A trained professional can spot the cause that is leading to the effect. Just as important, a professional can give you a cure to correct the flaw, as opposed to another flaw that will temporarily mask the first one. A few minutes with a professional can get you back on track. Trying to solve the problem yourself is a little like representing yourself in court. How does the old saying go? A man who serves as his own lawyer has a fool for a client.

I suppose it's just human nature, but we all have a tendency to practice the things we already do pretty well. In truth, we should do just the opposite if we hope to improve. Take sand shots. They're the scariest shots for most people, yet how often do you ever see anyone grinding away in a practice bunker? Not often.

The same holds true for putting. It accounts for about half the strokes in a round, but how many people do you ever see working on their putting?

While I'm on the subject of putting, here are two drills I do that can help you become a better putter.

The first drill is a confidence builder, and I think confidence is the most important single factor in becoming a good putter. I begin by placing three balls about three feet from the hole, and I putt from that distance until I make all three putts. Then I move back another couple of feet and repeat the drill. I keep this up until I'm hitting 15-footers, which is the limit for putts I realistically expect to make. It does wonders for my confidence to see those putts rolling into the hole, one after another, time after time.

The second drill helps me develop a feel for distance, which I think is more important than direction, especially on longer putts.

Rather than putting to a hole, I'll practice hitting putts to the fringe. By doing this, I'm focusing completely on distance rather than concerning myself with getting the ball into the hole. Direction becomes secondary, and this drill allows me really to concentrate on my stroke.

I have just a final thought on practicing. Depending on your schedule, it's a good idea to try to practice when there aren't a lot of people around. This is a time to concentrate, and that's hard to do when your friends are there and what you're really dying to do is catch up on all the juicy gossip. It's not easy to be disciplined enough to resist the temptation. It all comes down to just how much you want to improve—and how big a price you're willing to pay.

Lopez File: Laura Baugh

Laura had already been on the tour for four years when I finally turned pro, but of course, I already knew a lot about her.

Laura was like a dream come true for the tour. Not only was she beautiful and outgoing, but she could really play. Anyone who wins that U.S. Amateur at age 16 knows what she's doing on the golf course.

Maybe it's the fates, or just bad luck, but in 13 seasons Laura has come up with 10 second-place finishes but no titles. How else can you figure it? She has all the talent in the world, and believe me, she really, really wants to win. I watch her play, and she tries unbelievably hard on every shot.

I know that if Laura had gotten that first win under her belt early, things would have been a lot different. But I wonder now whether she'll ever win. For one thing, the pressure she puts on herself is staggering. For another, I just don't know if she can win playing a reduced schedule as she does. She loves being at home, being a good mom to her daughter Chelsea, but I've learned that no matter how much talent you have, you have to be out there playing to be truly competitive.

I also wonder if Laura even has the strength to play four solid rounds. She's small to begin with, and while she has a model's figure, I'm not sure that's the best build for competitive golf. Believe me, nobody has fought the battle of the scales harder or more often than I, but there's a limit to how much weight you can lose and still have the strength to play.

I've often wondered whether deep down inside, Laura has the killer instinct necessary to win. I look at JoAnne, Amy, Patty Sheehan, and some of the other players, and I just know that they come to win, not just to play. I don't see that in Laura, and I'm not sure it's something you can learn. I think it's a God-given gift.

I don't mean all this to sound hard on Laura, because I do admire her. She's as resilient a player as we have on tour. She never gets down on herself. She's never given up. And in a very real sense, maybe that's as important as winning golf tournaments.

It's certainly a good lesson for everyone.

8

Course Strategy: Thinking Your Way to Good Golf

All the talent in the world doesn't count for much if a person plays dumb golf. Taking unnecessary risks, playing toward the trouble on a hole, or not even taking the time to read a hole are all ingredients for a high score.

I've played with a lot of people who have all the shots but really don't have a clue about how to play golf. In a lot of ways, golf is like chess. You need to think one, two, or even three moves ahead while you calculate the shot you want to hit. You have to know how to play the percentages, how to judge when you need to gamble, and when you should back off and play safe, conservative golf.

There's an old saying that "golf is 75 percent mental." I'd say it's at least that much, and probably more. In this chapter we'll cover the mental side, and I think that it will help you lower your scores in a hurry. After all, not everybody has the physical ability to change his or her golf swing, or to learn new shots, but I do believe we can all learn to think better on the course.

READING THE COURSE
Seeing—and Avoiding—Trouble

One of my criteria for a good golf course is that it be straightforward. I don't mean it needs to be 18 holes without a dogleg. I mean that players shouldn't have any surprises or tricks awaiting them. I like to stand on a tee and see exactly where the problems and dangers are on a hole. That's the reason good players hate blind shots. They add an element of doubt and unnecessary risk to a game that's already difficult enough.

Standing on the tee, I begin my read of the hole by checking to make sure that the tee actually aims toward the center of the fairway. Occasionally, when a hole is redesigned, the tee will angle away from the center of the fairway. That means that if you aim perfectly and hit a good drive, you may still find yourself in the rough. This is even more crucial if the hole requires you to drive the ball through a chute of trees. If the tee is misaligned, you run the risk of driving into the trees.

My next decision is where I want to tee the ball. If the hole doglegs, I want to tee away from the dogleg in order to open up the

hole. I want to give myself the biggest possible target. The same holds true if I want to fade or draw the ball off the tee. If I'm going to draw the ball, I'll tee the ball on the left side of the tee and start the ball down the right side of the hole. I'll do just the opposite for a fade. The idea is to give myself the widest possible margin for error.

Now I'll look down the fairway to see where the trouble is. I want to steer away from either water or out-of-bounds stakes, since these are two-shot mistakes. If these aren't a factor, I look for fairway bunkers and the width of the landing area. Occasionally the course architect or tournament officials will try to trick you. They'll set up the hole to tempt you to drive over the bunkers, but they'll narrow the fairway beyond the bunkers to try to negate the advantage of a longer drive. Either that, or the hole will be short enough to begin with so that it's not worth the risk of driving into the bunkers.

Whatever the trouble, I make it a point to block it out of my mind before I get ready to hit the ball. The good player sees only the place he or she wants the ball to land. The poor player sees only the place he or she is afraid it might land—and the place it usually does.

If the hole is a dogleg, it presents another set of problems.

First, you have to decide whether it's worth trying to cut the corner in order to have a shorter second shot. This requires you to study the hole and see how much trouble you can get into if you take that route. How thick are the trees? Is the corner guarded by a bunker? If you drive into the bunker, can you reach the green? Is the corner protected by water or out-of-bounds? Finally, can you really shave enough off the dogleg to make the risks worthwhile? If it's going to mean only one club less on your approach, but you run the risk of a bogey or double bogey, it's a pretty dubious play.

Second, make sure you know the distance to the far side of the fairway and what happens if you drive the ball too far. Let's say I have 220 yards to the edge of the fairway, and I can hit my driver 240 yards. I have to ask myself whether I should try to work a driver around the dogleg or hit a 3-wood off the tee and guard against driving the ball through the fairway. If there's deep rough or woods or other dangers on the other side of the fairway, the smart play is to hit the 3-wood and take the danger out of play.

Having determined where the trouble is, my next consideration is where I can drive the ball to best set up my next shot, whether that's a putt on a par three, an approach to a par four or short par five, or my second shot on a longer par five.

If I'm trying to set up my approach, I want to know where the pin is placed. That's why it's always a good idea to check any pin placements you can as you play adjacent holes. It's a small edge but one that can really help.

Once I know where the pin is, I want to determine the safest approach. Again, is water or out-of-bounds a factor? If so, I want to play away from them, since those are two-shot mistakes. Then I look for bunkers. I want to avoid the bunkers, but I particularly want to avoid bunkers that are near the hole because if I should get a bad lie in the bunker and find I can't spin the ball and stop it quickly, that gives me less green to work with. Finally, I want to know what is behind the green. If there's deep rough, or if it falls away sharply, I know that's a place to avoid. Very often a course architect will try to fool you by putting trouble in front of the green to try to lure you into playing to the back, only to find the trouble behind the green is twice as bad—a two-shot mistake instead of a one-shot error.

Once I know where the trouble is, and the best route to avoid it, I want to check the slope of the green. If it slopes severely from either front to back or side to side, or if it falls off in the back, I need to know how to plan accordingly. On most greens, particularly fast greens, it's a smart play to leave your approach below the hole. This allows you to putt uphill, negating the speed of the green and giving yourself an easier putt. This strategy is particularly important on greens that slope away on the back edge. There's not much advantage in firing at a pin cut on the back third of the green, only to watch it roll off the back edge and trickle into a rough—or worse.

If possible, also watch the approach shots hit by your playing companions. These will give you some idea of the firmness of the greens, as well as how the ball will run as it approaches the hole. If a green is firm, it doesn't make sense to try to fly the ball at the hole, only to watch it carom off the green.

Now it's time to figure out what kind of shot I can play. That's when the lie, wind, and weather conditions come into play.

The lie of the ball determines what kind of shot you can play. If it's in the rough, you are going to catch a flier. Grass will come between the clubface and the ball, and it will come out without much spin, much like a spitball in a baseball. The ball will fly farther than a shot hit off the fairway, and it won't check up on the green, so allow for plenty of roll. The same thing will happen in wet weather, because a film of water will come between the clubface and the ball. Also, keep in mind that because you can't spin the ball, it's very difficult either to fade or to draw the ball, so don't even try. It's a sickening feeling to aim the ball at a greenside bunker and plan either to fade or to draw it into the green, only to watch as it never moves off the bunker and is buried in the sand.

If the ball is sitting down in the fairway, it also limits your options. The more the ball is sitting down, the less you'll be able to do. That's why good players prefer to play on short, bent-grass fairways. The ball sits up perfectly, and they can pull off miracles. Balls tend to sit down a little more in Bermuda or bluegrass fairways.

Climate is the next consideration. If the air is heavy, the ball won't fly as far. That's why shots travel farther in a place like Denver than they will in Miami, where the air is heavier, and why the wind affects shots more in humid climates.

The wind is a big factor in the shot you'll be able to hit. There are two schools of thought about playing in a crosswind. Some people prefer to hang the ball out in the wind and let the wind bring it back to the target. Others prefer to hold shots against the wind.

In other words, if the wind is blowing from right to left, they'll hit a fade and try to get the ball to hold its line against the wind. A third option, if the green isn't bunkered in front, is to hit the knockdown shot, punching the ball low and under the wind and letting it run up to the hole.

I think it comes down to what the risks are, how strong the wind is, and how confident you are in your shotmaking that day. If you're not confident in hitting just the right amount of fade or draw, it's probably a better risk just to hang the ball out in the wind and let it go for a ride. Again, it all comes down to a question of instinct and confidence.

A headwind is a shotmaker's dream. If the wind is blowing toward you, it will increase the backspin on the ball, and the ball will check up more quickly when it lands. By the same token, if you have to play a shot downwind, don't count on much spin, and allow for more roll. And remember, if you are planning to nip a wedge and try for a shot that comes in checking, it will work better if the green slopes toward you. You can kiss that shot good-bye on a green that falls away from you.

Finally, now that I know where the trouble is, and the shot I need to hit for the best approach, I want to figure out where the best place is to miss the shot. Remember, the one absolute reality in golf is that it is a game of misses. You are going to miss, if only slightly, more shots than you are going to hit perfectly.

First, you want to avoid shooting at what I call "sucker pins." Those are pins tucked into almost impossible places where the risks far outweigh the rewards. Unless it's the closing holes of a tournament, and I absolutely must have a birdie, I'll play to the fat part of the green, leaving open the possibility of picking up a stroke but virtually eliminating the chances of dropping one to a bogey.

If I have to attack the hole, I want to stack as many odds in my favor as possible. Let me give you an example. I've come to the 71st hole of a tournament. I'm one shot off the lead, but the final hole is a long, difficult par five that I can't reach in two. That means I must birdie this hole to have any realistic hope of forcing a playoff.

The hole is a 165-yard par three. The pin is cut eight paces from the left edge of the green, with deep bunkers guarding both sides of the green, which falls off sharply in the back, down to a small creek. On top of all that, the wind is blowing from left to right. It's not a strong wind, but it is a steady wind. The green is wide but not particularly firm, slightly elevated, and slopes gently

from back to front until it reaches a crest about a third of the way from the front edge, where it breaks off sharply.

In a normal situation, I'd take a 6-iron and hit a smooth shot to the center of the green. If anything, I might cut it a little to help make sure the ball sits down quickly and doesn't run off the back edge. I'll take both bunkers out of play and still leave myself an uphill putt and a fairly routine par.

Knowing I must birdie the hole, I run through my checklist:

Trouble—The worst trouble is behind the green, in the water or the rough. The water is a two-shot mistake, and I'm dead. I might get a decent lie in the rough, but the green falls away from me, and unless I hit the pin, I don't have much of a chance of stopping the ball near the hole to save par.

The next-worst place to be is the left-hand bunker, because it is so close to the pin. I may get lucky and get a good lie, but again, it's not realistic to think that I can stop the ball on a downslope no matter how much spin I can put on the ball.

The right-hand bunker isn't much of a bargain either, but it does have a couple of advantages. First, I have more green to work with. If the ball should bury, I can still get it out and let it run toward the hole. Second, in all likelihood I'll leave myself with an uphill putt, which is a little easier on the nerves on fast greens.

The Lie—Perfect.

The Wind—Moderate but steady from left to right. I constantly check the trees, near both the green and the tee, to make sure the wind isn't swirling or gusting. It's fairly humid, so the wind will be a definite factor.

The Green—The greens have been holding pretty well all day, but as the wind has picked up in the afternoon the greens have become slightly firmer. I make it a point to watch my playing companions' shots and notice that they check up fairly well.

The Shot—In order to get the ball close, I have four options:

1. A 6-iron, straight at the hole—A 165-yard shot is right about in the middle of my 6-iron range. Even though the hole is slightly uphill, I want to guard against getting above the hole and leaving myself a downhill putt. The problem is the pin position. Since the wind is blowing from left to right, I must start the ball to the left of the pin and let the wind blow it back to the hole if I'm going to get the ball close. I could start it right at the hole, figuring that even if the ball hangs out to the right I'm OK. But if the ball draws slightly, I've lost my margin for error on the left, and I could

well dump the ball into the bunker and face an almost impossible up and down to save par.

2. A knockdown 5-iron—I could try to take the wind out of the picture altogether by hitting a low 5-iron and letting it run up to the hole. The green is open in front, so there are no front bunkers to contend with. There are two problems with this shot. First, because of the ridge a third of the way up the green, I run the risk of driving the ball into the ridge and killing the shot, leaving me with a long, uphill putt. Hardly the stuff birdies are made of. An even worse possibility is that the ball might not come out low enough and could run over the green, into the rough and possibly the water.

3. Fade a 6-iron—I'm comfortable hitting a fade, and it has the benefit of being a shot that will sit down quickly once it hits the green. Since a fade won't carry as far as a draw, I have a good chance of staying below the hole, as well as getting close enough for a realistic birdie.

Here are the problems with this shot: First, to get close to the pin I'd have to start the ball out over the bunker, even if there wasn't any wind. With the wind, it means I might even have to start the ball to the left of the bunker. By doing this, I bring the entire bunker into play and basically take the safe part of the green out of play altogether.

Second, even though I'm comfortable hitting a fade, there's always the chance that under pressure I won't quite pull it off. If that happens, I'm either left of the bunker, facing an impossible pitch out of the rough; in the bunker; or above the hole, facing a downhill putt. I don't like my odds with this shot.

4. Draw a 7-iron—The hole, at 165 yards, is a little outside the range of my normal 7-iron, but since I plan to bring the shot from right to left, I know that it will be a stronger shot and will carry a little farther, but probably not far enough to get me either above the hole or over the green. Also, under pressure, you tend to get pumped up and hit the ball farther than normal. By dropping down to a 7-iron, I can go ahead and put a good swing on the ball, knowing that unless something freaky happens, I've taken the worst of the trouble—the stuff behind the green—out of the picture.

To get the ball close, I must start the ball out to the right of the flag and draw it back in. That's OK, though, because all I'm going to do is start the ball over the middle, or maybe the right middle of the green, and draw it into the pin. This means that I've taken both bunkers out of play. There's not much chance of my drawing the ball far enough to get in the left-hand bunker, and unless I practically shank the shot, the ball should never even get close to the right-hand bunker.

The wind isn't much of a factor, since I'll be working the ball against the wind. If anything, it helps protect me from hitting the ball into the left-hand bunker. In fact, since I'm drawing the ball into the wind, I'm actually turning it into a headwind, which, coupled with the relatively soft, uphill green, will help the ball check up more quickly than it ordinarily might.

This is the shot I want to play. I know where I want to hit it— right on the flag—and, more important, I know that if I miss it I'm still putting uphill from no farther than the middle of the green. It's still a risky shot, but I've taken as much risk as possible out of it.

Oh, naturally the shot comes off perfectly. I run in a six-footer for birdie, then go on to win the greatest playoff in U.S. Women's Open history.

Well, this is my book, right?

LAYING UP
Knowing When . . . and How

There are times when you simply must lay up short of the hole. Maybe you just can't hit the ball far enough. Maybe your lie won't let you try for the green. Or maybe there's just too much trouble around the green to make going for it a smart play. I know that I have a hard and fast rule. If I have to play a shot over water, I won't even try it unless I can clear the water with a 4-wood. I don't ever want to have to count on hitting a perfect 3-wood to clear the hazard.

In any case, you want to make sure that you take three factors into consideration when you decide to lay up.

First, if you are going to lay up, then make sure you really do lay up. I remember playing in a tournament and coming to a hole with water in the landing area. I left my driver in the bag, took out a 3-wood, and drove the ball into the water. I was so pumped up that I hit the ball farther than normal. I had the right idea, but in all the excitement I hadn't taken my adrenaline into consideration, and I paid the price. It hasn't happened since, believe me.

Second, you want to make sure you leave yourself with the best approach to the green. Study the situation and try to find a spot to lay up that is well away from any trouble and will give you an easy shot at the hole.

Third, lay back far enough to give yourself a full shot with either a sand wedge or a pitching wedge. Too often I see players hit the ball as close as possible to the green, only to find themselves with a delicate little pitch shot. When I lay up, I try to leave myself about 50 yards to the flag, since that lets me take an aggressive swing with my sand wedge and put plenty of spin on the ball.

Lopez File: Jan Stephenson

My gosh, what can I say about Jan? I sometimes think my life has been a little like a soap opera, but Jan has had moments that are right out of "General Hospital."

When Jan first came on tour, she and Laura Baugh got a lot of attention because they were so pretty. People would follow them just to look at them. The fact that they played pretty good golf was secondary.

It's no secret that some of the other players resented this, and they didn't take any great pains to keep their feelings to themselves. The roof really blew off when Jan posed one year for our tour magazine, *Fairway*. Let's just say that the photo proved beyond a doubt that there's nothing wrong with her thighs. Jane Blalock and some of the others ripped into Jan and the tour. It seems to me that the phrase "quasi-pornographic" was used, which was a little extreme. I always felt that JoAnne Carner had the best attitude about the entire business. She just told the press, "I wish someone had asked me to pose."

At any rate, Jan just smiled a lot, gave a lot of interviews, and made quite a name for herself, which was fine with her and fine with the tour.

Lost in all the excitement was the fact that Jan was one of the hardest workers out here. She would grind for hours on the practice tee. It all paid off, and her record shows 14 wins, including the 1983 U.S. Women's Open and two of our other major championships.

Since 1984 Jan hasn't won very often, and I think she's lost a lot of confidence in her putting and a little of the desire that made her such a good player. Maybe she's just a little tired of the tour and is looking at other outside activities. I can understand that.

Jan has managed to stay in the public eye, so to speak. Over the last few years she's done calendars that show plenty of, uh, enthusiasm for the Dunlop golf balls she's promoting. Let's just say I don't imagine Janie Blalock and some of the other girls are a whole lot happier with Jan and her calendars than they were a few years ago.

I really like Jan. A couple of years ago we did a press conference together, and someone asked about the calendars. Jan said she was shocked that Dunlop used only some of the sexier shots. She insisted that she wanted to be known as "a player, not as a sweater girl."

All I know is, there are still a lot of guys in her galleries who wouldn't know a 5-iron from a monkey wrench, so she must be doing something right.

As for what you can learn from Jan's game, I guess it was her willingness to work so hard to make herself a good player. Most people talk a lot about working hard on their games. What they really do is talk a good practice session.

9

Getting Out of Trouble: The Fine Art of Damage Control

Once I got good enough to compete in tournaments, my father told me something that I always keep in mind on the course. "Nancy," he said, "to win you must avoid double bogeys. You can always get the stroke back when you make a bogey, because you'll always make your share of birdies. But eagles are hard to come by, and nobody's share of birdies is big enough to make up for many double bogeys."

That really struck home when Ray began to play golf. He'd hit the ball into trouble, then try shots that were not only odds-defying, some were almost death-defying.

Ray made the mistake that a lot of players make. He counted on miracle shots when he should have been playing the percentages. Rather than just getting the ball back into play, he would try to hit it between branches, under shrubs, or over trees. Most of the time he'd just get the ball in deeper trouble, and instead of making a bogey he'd be on his way to double figures.

Ray is a third baseman for the Orioles, and as we played I explained the whole business of playing from trouble in baseball terms. I said: "It's like you're trying to hold a runner on third. First and second base are open, and there's one out. The batter hits a hard grounder to you, and you make a diving catch to stop the ball from bouncing into left field. But instead of being satisfied with holding the runner on third, you try to scramble to your feet and make a great throw to first base. Whoops. It's almost an impossible throw, the ball sails over the first baseman, and both runners advance."

Well, of course that made perfect sense to Ray. Even in that split second he would have instinctively made the percentage play, held the ball, and hoped to turn a double play on the next batter to get out of the inning.

Too often golfers try impossible shots when it isn't necessary. That leads to my first rule: unless you absolutely have to save par, accept your one-shot mistake and play for bogey, pitching the ball back into the fairway safely.

When I do hit the ball into trouble, the first thing I do is check my lie. That will determine just how tricky a shot I'll be able to try. If I have a bad lie, it forces me to hit the safest shot possible.

Once I've checked the lie, I look at my alternatives. With a perfect lie, I know I can hit a high shot. If it's less than perfect, I'm forced to punch or chip the ball back into play.

Once I pick the opening I want to play to, and have a feel for the shot I want to hit, I make sure to check the area I'm hitting to. If there's water or out-of-bounds through the fairway, you can be sure my ball will not be coming out of the woods with much heat on it. There is nothing dumber than hitting a great recovery shot, only to have it keep running into even worse trouble.

Whatever shot you decide on, the most important thing is to get the ball out of trouble. There are a lot of would-be heroes running around with 30 handicaps.

Lopez File: Beth Daniel

When Beth came out on tour in 1979, a lot of people predicted she was going to be the next great, dominant player. That wasn't exactly going out on a limb, since Beth had won the U.S. Women's Amateur in 1975 and 1976 and had been a dominant player on two Curtis Cup teams and a World Amateur team.

Sure enough, in her first year she won a tournament and almost $100,000. For the next two years she led the money list with over $200,000 in winnings. She had a fierce competitive attitude, and her swing was perfectly suited to her tall, lanky body. At 5 feet, 11 inches, she was able to take advantage of her height to generate a lot of power. Unlike shorter players, she was able to hit the ball both high and far, which is the ideal combination. On top of all that, she had a short game that she could count on under the gun.

While she has won 14 tournaments, the past few seasons have been disappointing for Beth. She's had some back problems, which have hurt. It may be because of her back, but I've noticed a change not only in her swing but also in her approach to playing. Beth was always a very natural player, but now she seems much more mechanical. I think that must be very difficult, because it works against what seems right or normal. Sometimes I wonder if Beth is going through a period of confusion in her game.

I remember going through a similar period early in my third year on tour. I had gotten married that winter, and a lot of things seemed more important than working on my golf. My swing fell totally apart. I got very flat at the top of the backswing, and that was only one of the bad swing habits I fell into.

The more I tried to figure out what was wrong, the more complicated things became, until finally I was a wreck. I was looking at pictures and tapes of my swing, worrying about this and that, and for the first time in my career, really having some severe doubts about my swing and game—and maybe even my future in golf. I hit rock bottom in one tournament when I shot an 83. An 83! I hadn't shot a round that high since I was a kid, and the truth is, I had to play my tail off to score that well.

Finally, my dad came to the rescue. He listened to all the mechanical and theoretical mumbo jumbo I had been thinking about, and said, "That's very nice, Nancy," and then told me to empty out my brain and just hit the ball. Period. Just step up and hit it.

It was like magic. I just put my swing on cruise control, and everything returned to normal.

Maybe that won't work for Beth. Once you've struggled for a while, you have to be pretty lucky to get out of it as easily as I did. Golf is a difficult game, but it's a little easier if you trust your instincts. It's too hard a game to try to play like someone else.

10

Being a Competitor: Playing to Win . . . and Have Fun

Earlier we covered the mechanics that will help you hit better golf shots, as well as the thinking and planning that will help you shoot better scores. I honestly believe these areas will help almost every golfer improve.

But in this chapter I want to deal with being a competitor, and I have to say right from the beginning that I'm not sure being a good competitor is something you can learn. I often have the feeling that it's a God-given talent that some people have and others never will.

I can't give you a step-by-step routine to help you become a competitor, as I could to tell you how to hit a sand shot. But I think that if you honestly look at your attitudes toward competition after you read this chapter, it might give you some valuable insights.

A MATTER OF PRIDE

If there is one characteristic that all great champions share, it's an enormous sense of pride. That's true in all walks of life. The people who excel are those who are driven to show the world—and prove to themselves—just how good they are.

It may seem like a small thing, but did you ever see a great player who looked like a dirtbag? I've never seen one. All the great players I've seen keep themselves in good shape, are well groomed, and dress nicely. It's a matter of self-image. If you look good, you'll feel good about yourself, and that can't help carrying over into your golf—or any other endeavor.

I know that I can't play well if I don't think I look good. That's one very pragmatic reason that I've made it a point to get my weight back to normal after giving birth to both Ashley and Erinn. My father always used to kid me, saying, "10 more pounds, 10 more yards," but enough was enough!

It also carries over to equipment. I need to have spotless clubs in order to play my best. I sometimes play with people who have so much dirt and grass on their clubs that it's a wonder they ever hit a solid shot. Again, I think it's a matter of pride, and more often than not, most golfers I see with equipment in that condition don't have much pride in their game.

Still, looking nice and having well-kept clubs are just a small part of having pride. True competitors love the challenge of putting their pride on the line and responding. As I look back on my career, I know I've played my best golf when my pride was either hurt or challenged—by either another player or the situation. And that's true for all great players. Look at Sam Snead and Ben Hogan. They brought out the best in each other's game when they went head-to-head. Or how about Jack Nicklaus when another player came along to challenge his domination of the men's tour? Think of the classic rivalries he had over the years with Arnold Palmer, Lee Trevino, Johnny Miller, and Tom Watson. It wasn't anything personal. It's just that when the starter says, "Play away," your pride is on the line and the game is on. I know that, for me, that's when golf is really the most fun.

I can think of plenty of times when I felt I had something to prove and couldn't wait to get out and prove it. Earlier I talked about the time JoAnne Carner said she was going to "leave me in the dust" at the Golden Lights tournament in New York. I went on to win, and it was one of the wins in my streak of five straight in 1978. I learned a lot about being a competitor during that streak.

I'm not a believer in false modesty, and when I came out on tour I knew I was good. But until I got on that streak in 1978, I didn't really appreciate just how good a player I was. It was like the rest of the tour just stood still. It's a funny thing about a streak, but it has a snowball effect. I was playing well, so my confidence was high. Because I was so confident, my concentration level was very high, and I didn't let little things distract me. It also meant that I could finesse more shots than I ordinarily would. And last but not least, because I was playing so well, the other players were looking over their shoulders, worrying about what I was going to do next. All the pieces were falling into place. I didn't have room for any negative thoughts. All I knew was that I was playing well and loving every minute of it. Anyone who was going to stop my streak was going to have to deal with one mad little Mexican in the final round. My pride was on the line.

Eventually, of course, my streak did end. Nobody can sustain a concentration level that high for that long. And after five weeks I was physically and mentally tired. But something else happened along the way. I noticed that the other players lifted the level of their game. Their pride was on the line as well, and toward the end of that magical five weeks I could no longer go out and win with par on the last day.

Several years later, at the 1985 LPGA Championship, I got as mad as I've ever been on the golf course, but instead of letting my anger destroy my chances in the tournament I made it work to my advantage, which is something I think all good competitors manage to do.

Playing in the third round, I was paired with Janet Coles and Chris Johnson. Both were struggling through difficult rounds, while I was playing the best round of my career. Usually it's pretty hard to shoot a good score when your playing companions are grinding. Play is slower than you'd like, and it's tough to concentrate, especially when the other players are hitting the ball all over the lot, and you have to wait for rulings.

Sure enough, on our 12th hole the officials came out to tell us we had fallen 27 minutes behind the previous group and that we were going to be timed. That only added to the pressure, because we

were very conscious that we had just 45 seconds for each shot, no matter how difficult.

Still, coming into the closing holes, I was on my way to an outstanding score that might put the tournament out of reach. On the 7th hole—which was really our 16th hole—I knocked my approach three inches from the cup for a birdie.

Pumped up, I hit a good 4-iron on the next hole, a par three, and made par. As I walked off the green the officials told me I'd taken 86 seconds on that shot and was going to be penalized.

I couldn't believe it. The greatest round of my life, and I'm being penalized for slow play. First of all, it's not even my fault we're out of position, and second of all, there's no living way that shot took almost a minute and a half to play. As hard as I tried not to, I broke down in tears of anger and frustration. Chris and Janet felt terrible, but there wasn't anything they could do.

Standing on the final tee, I could barely see the ball through the tears. Somehow I hit a good drive, hit my approach to six feet, and parred out. Without the penalty strokes I would have shot a 63.

The next day I had tunnel vision. I don't remember anything about anyone else's round. I don't remember the galleries. I don't remember the television cameras or anything else. All I knew was that I was going to show the LPGA and its officials and its rulings that I could win in spite of them all. I promise you, nobody could have beaten me that day. Nothing could have happened that would have cost me that tournament. I got into a zone where I could see every shot before I hit it, and every shot was perfect in my mind.

I got more satisfaction from that win than any other before or since. And I doubt that if I win another 100 tournaments, any of them will ever give me as much pure satisfaction.

The point I want to make is that a competitor will find a way to win. Competitors take bad breaks and use them to drive themselves just that much harder. Quitters take bad breaks and use them as reasons to give up. It's all a matter of pride.

CONCENTRATION

People often ask me whether I think Ashley and Erinn will become good golfers. I think it's a little early to tell, but I do know that at age four Ashley concentrates a lot better than most kids her age. If she is looking at a book, the world can fall apart around her and she'll still be looking at that book. When I take her to the golf course, she'll take her little club and focus as hard as she can on whacking the ball. Nobody will ever accuse her of having a swing like Mickey Wright's, but then nobody's saying her mother does either.

The ability to concentrate is a characteristic all good competitors must have. You need to be able to focus fully on each shot, one shot at a time. You can't get too high or too low about the previous shot or hole. And you can't worry about what's going to happen two holes from now. You have to live in the present on the course.

Whenever people talk about competitors with great concentration, Ben Hogan's name comes up. According to one story, he was paired with Claude Harmon in the Masters one year when Harmon aced the par-three 12th. The large gallery went wild; the roar was enormous.

As they walked to the next tee, Hogan turned to Harmon and asked, "Claude, what did you make there?"

"Why Ben, I made a one," said a startled Harmon.

"Oh," said Hogan and wrote the figure on his scorecard.

Now that's concentrating! I don't think many people can concentrate that well. I'm not even sure they should try. But for the minute or so that it takes to plan a shot, address the ball, and hit it, I think your game deserves your undivided attention.

My concentration was severely tested in Rochester in 1978. I was going for my fifth straight win, and things weren't going very well in the final round. I had been hooking the ball badly off the tee for the entire front nine and was struggling.

As I stood on the 10th tee, the large gallery stretched down both sides of the hole. Instead of hooking the ball, I hit it straight right, hitting a spectator on the head and knocking him to the ground. There was blood all over the place.

"Oh, my gosh," I said, as my heart pounded and I raced to see how badly he was hurt.

"Oh, please stay in bounds," said my caddie, Roscoe, who apparently didn't have any problems with his concentration.

The spectator, Dr. Gerry Mesollela, said he was fine and urged me to get back out and play. I was so shaken, I wasn't sure I'd ever be able to hit another ball, much less play again.

I double-bogeyed the hole and didn't see any way I could regroup. Winning the tournament was the furthest thing from my mind. All I could see was the blood.

As I walked to the next tee, I made a deal with myself. I decided to dedicate the tournament to Gerry. Once I did that, I was able to put the accident out of my mind and concentrate on the job at hand. Sure enough, I won, and Gerry has been a good friend ever since.

COMPETITION AND FRIENDSHIP

Everybody likes to win, or so they say. The truth of the matter is that some people shy away from really turning on the heat because they're afraid they might lose friends if they keep beating them. I can't say I've ever worried much about that, but I know it happens.

Successful competitors want to win. Head cases want to win at all costs. Those are the people who would cheat, cut corners, or run over their grandmothers just to get their name on a silver cup. Competitors just want to go out there, do their best, and shake hands when it's all over.

It all comes down to a question of priorities. When I'm on the course, it's my job to concentrate fully, do my best, and try to win. If the person I happen to beat is a friend, I have to hope he or she realizes that it's nothing personal. We're both out there for the same reason. If you lose a friend because you've won fair and square, that person probably wasn't much of a friend to begin with.

Jo Ann Washam is one of my best friends on tour. Early in my career we'd occasionally room together to save on expenses.

On one occasion, we came into the final round at Costa Mesa paired in the last group. Things weren't what you'd call tense in the room Saturday night, but the atmosphere wasn't as relaxed as it normally would be. Both of us knew that, if we were going to win, we had to beat the other player. If we went out and played like friends, someone else would come along and beat us both. I wanted to win. If I didn't, I wanted Jo Ann to win. I sure didn't want someone else to come along and win because we were too worried about each other.

Jo Ann and I talked about it and decided that we'd try to act like we weren't friends when we got to the course. That worked until we walked off the first tee; then I couldn't stand it any longer.

"Jo Ann, this is just killing me," I said. "I have to know what you're thinking."

That was fine for a while, but things did tighten up on the final nine. She had me by two shots with four holes to play. I went birdie-birdie and finally won.

I went back to the room with mixed feelings. I was glad I had won, but I felt badly that I had to beat Jo Ann to do it. The hard

truth is that, no matter how much you might like someone, once you tee it up, your friends become acquaintances until the last putt is holed. That may sound cold, but that's the toughest part of being a competitor.

And that's where your soul-searching has to begin.

Lopez File: Some Players to Watch

So far we've talked about some familiar faces in these short player sketches, but there are a lot of good players out there who will be getting their share of headlines in the years to come. This seems like a pretty good time to take a look at them, too.

Jane Geddes

Photo courtesy of Robert Walker.

I guess a lot of people were surprised when Jane won the 1986 U.S. Women's Open, but I really wasn't because Jane has both the game and the temperament to go out and win the big tournaments.

I first played with her in the 1986 Henredon Classic, and even though her game hadn't developed fully, I could see she was going to be a good player. Jane has that rare ability to concentrate very hard on the job at hand and yet stay relaxed under pressure. She's also very aggressive but plays within herself. There's a big difference between being aggressive and being foolish.

It's a funny thing about the Women's Open. We've had 11 players come out and make it their first tournament win, and yet many of them have had limited success since then. Jane didn't waste any time proving that wasn't going to be the case with her. She's already won several times since the Open, and there's no doubt that she'll continue to be a winner, year in and year out.

Like Julie Inkster, Jane is a player who is aggressive but chooses the right spots to let loose and attack a course. I think everyone can learn a lot about how this game should be played by watching the players on our tour, and course management is one of the best lessons we can teach. Watching Jane, people can see a textbook example of when to use power to try to get an edge on the course and when to settle wisely for par and walk away quietly.

Betsy King

Photo courtesy of Robert Walker.

Betsy is a player I would describe as "sneaky good." She finished second on the money list last year, but that went largely unnoticed because Pat Bradley had such a great year. Betsy was an outstanding amateur, but she played for Furman University at the same time Beth Daniel was there, so you know who got all the attention.

In a way, you couldn't blame Betsy if she felt a little like Rodney Dangerfield. No matter what she does, she "don't get no respect."

That's not really true, of course. She's an outstanding athlete, ranking right up there with Patty Sheehan as one of the best pure athletes on tour. She's also a great putter; in fact, I'd say she's easily one of the five best on tour.

Someone asked me a while back what I thought of Betsy's game, and I said I thought she played just like she is, shy. I don't mean that she's timid on the course. She's a very smart player who knows when it's time to take a chance. I mean that she's very unemotional, almost businesslike, the same way Pat Bradley is on the course. If Betsy or Pat tried to play a wide-open, emotional game like Jo Anne Carner does, we might never hear from either one of them again.

Betsy has a quiet confidence, both in herself and in her game. I see this come out in competition. You can just see her set her teeth and go to work on the job at hand. She doesn't let either good shots or bad breaks affect her, but instead she seems to get in a zone of perfect concentration.

The majority of golfers aren't blessed with Betsy King's athletic ability. And for darn sure, there aren't a lot of people running around who can putt like she can. But I think everyone can take a lesson from her ability to concentrate and her willingness just to be herself on the golf course.

Sally Little

Photo courtesy of Robert Walker.

Sally has been out on tour since 1971 and has won 14 tournaments in her career. That doesn't give a true indication of just how good a player she really is. She's had to suffer through abdominal surgery as well as surgery on a knee, and both of those operations took their toll on her career. She sent a signal that she was back at the 1986 U.S. Women's Open when she tied with Jane Geddes, only to lose in a very close playoff.

Sally plays with a lot of grace. She's got a beautiful tempo. In fact, she's one of those players people like to play with because they unconsciously find themselves copying her tempo.

Maybe it's because she's been through so much surgery, or because she had to leave her home in South Africa to come to the States, but whatever the reason, Sally is one of the toughest players on tour. She's just incredibly strong mentally, and that counts for so much under pressure. I don't think I've ever seen her crack or heard her complain. She just plays the hand she's dealt the best she can.

Sally is very nice off the course, but on the course she bears down so hard that I hesitate even to talk to her. It's as though she just purses her lips and goes to war with the course. I think that's an awfully difficult way to play because it takes so much out of you.

I think that if Sally can stay injury-free, she'll be a player to reckon with for a long time out here. She's got all the shots. She's got a great touch around the greens, and most important, she's got the mental toughness to keep fighting while the majority of the field is giving up. That's an awfully tough combination to beat.

Patty Sheehan

Photo courtesy of Robert Walker.

Patty is the ultimate jock. Name a game, and Patty loves to play it. I don't think there's a sport she wouldn't be great in if she set her mind to it.

In a sense, Patty and I are a lot alike, in that we learned to play almost totally by athletic instincts and feel. I think it's safe to say that neither of us spends a lot of time worrying about the mechanics of the golf swing. I think that's one reason we've both been able to avoid prolonged slumps. If our swings aren't working, we're able to correct the problem through feel, rather than breaking our swings down and rebuilding them from scratch.

There's nobody more fun to watch than Patty when she's on a roll. If Pat Bradley and Betsy King keep their emotions to themselves, Patty tosses them out there for everyone to see. Winning or losing, there's never any doubt how Patty is feeling at the moment.

Patty is already one of the top players we have, and there's no question in my mind that she has the ability and the pure competitive instincts to be a Hall of Famer. I just wonder whether golf can hold her interest long enough. She goes through periods when she just doesn't want to play, and in that sense she reminds me a lot of Hollis Stacy.

People might look at Patty—or any of us for that matter—and wonder how we can get tired of golf. The money is good. The places we play are nice. There's not much heavy lifting, and you hardly ever get yelled at for messing something up. The truth is, it's not simply the golf that wears you out. It's the hassles of travelling and the mental exhaustion of concentrating on every shot for four straight days. Plus, after a while you begin to miss life in the real world.

Patty has established a home for troubled teenage girls called "Tigh Sheehan." That's a great thing for the girls, and it's also a great thing for Patty because it gives her a place to call home. It gives her a family and a place to center her life. It gives her a place in the real world where she can go and recuperate from the sometimes not-so-real world of the tour. It gives her a place to be Patty Sheehan, Human Being.

Laura Davies

Long-hitting Laura Davies from Great Britain was almost a legend on the LPGA tour before ever venturing out to play. We had heard from American Curtis Cup players of her immense power after the 1984 match. Mind you, we had heard these claims about other players and had always taken them with a pinch of salt. But when Laura showed up for the 1986 U.S. Open, it was pretty clear that the claims were far from exaggerated. With very little preparation, she finished in the top ten and it was obvious that there was plenty of potential for an American win. Like many overseas players, Laura was committed to her own country where the Women's Professional Golf Association obviously needed her talents. Then in 1987 Laura was back again for the U.S. Open and powered her way to victory in a play-off against JoAnne Carner and Ayako Okamoto.

JoAnne has always been thought of as one of the longest hitters in the women's game. But I think even she was a bit overwhelmed by Laura's enormous strength, her size and the truly vast distances she hits the ball. We really had seen nothing like it.

But what is great about Laura is that she also plays a totally attacking and fearless game like Seve Ballesteros. You ask yourself why she's taking risks with shots and not playing in a conservative way. But that just isn't Laura. If she can reach the green she'll have a go and if she doesn't make the green, well then she's got one of the finest short games in professional golf. I've seen her play some great sand shots and some really delicate pitches. Sometimes we tend to think that people who are large can be clumsy. But Laura obviously has the strength and control in her hands to play the most beautifully executed little shots around the green and her putting is delightfully reliable and sensitive.

I'm sure Laura will make a great go of things on the American LPGA tour. Fortunately, the Association decided to grant her her player's card without going to the tour school. As U.S. Open Champion there wasn't much argument that she should be out there playing. The crowds really warm to her. Although she is large and never going to be one of the outstanding glamour players on the tour she has a great smile, a real sense of humour and is obviously going to like the social side of tournaments!

It is also good for our American tour to have as many overseas players as possible. It means that the foreign newspapers and television stations start covering our events. Some of our leading players who are household names in the States forget that they aren't at all known overseas. People like Laura can only do us good and bring our tour more recognition around the world.

11

Exercise and Nutrition: Giving Yourself a Chance to Play Your Best

You can have all the talent in the world, but if your body is in bad shape, you won't be able to get the most out of your game. People don't ordinarily think of golf as a particularly athletic or demanding sport, but they are wrong. It takes strong arms to slash a ball out of the rough. It takes strong hands to hit those delicate little pitch shots around the greens. It takes strong legs to walk 18 holes, especially on a hilly course. And it takes good nerves to stand over a left-to-right-breaking three-footer when the match is on the line.

The truth is, you can really cut strokes off your score if you do some very simple exercises. You don't want big, heavy muscles, but you do want to be strong and supple. And you want to take care of your body by eating and drinking things that give you strength, not take it away.

GETTING IN SHAPE

Common sense will pretty much tell you what parts of your body need the most attention if you are going to play good golf. You need strong hands, arms, and legs. You also need to work on the back and abdominal muscles to avoid back injuries. The golf swing is a very stressful movement, particularly on the lower back. Here are some suggestions that might help you build up the right kind of strength for golf.

Hands

Some people might not like to hear this, but the one area where the golfers on the PGA Tour are better as a group than the players on our tour is around the greens. They just have better short games, and I think a big reason for that is the strength they have in their hands. I don't believe there has ever been a player with small, weak hands who had a good variety of shots around the greens. You need strength to make the delicate little movements that spell the difference between great shotmaking and simply being decent around the greens.

I'm blessed with unusually big, strong hands, and I've always had a good short game. The same is true for Pat Bradley and Jo Anne Carner. If you're not so lucky, here's what you can do.

First, anything you can do that requires hand strength is good exercise. Gardening is particularly good. I also recommend squeezing tennis balls or buying those grippers or hand springs that people use to build up their hands. Any sporting goods store will have them, but avoid the difficult ones in the beginning.

Whatever you do, remember that golf is a two-handed game, so pay equal attention to both hands. In fact, anything you can do to strengthen and increase the coordination in your "weaker" hand is a good idea. Even a little thing like brushing your teeth with your weaker hand will help.

Legs

If you are a person who rides in carts, you might wonder why you need to bother with strengthening your legs. Well, for starters, you *shouldn't* be riding in a cart; I think it hurts your game.

Leaving that aside, though, your legs need strength because they support your golf swing. They also help in the timing of the swing and

add power. If you don't think that's the case, try locking your knees and swinging stiff-legged. I think you'll get the point.

Walking is great exercise for golf. I'd love to run, but my feet are so bad that it's not possible. Instead, on days when I'm not playing I make it a point to walk at least two miles. And when I say *walk*, I'm not talking about a gentle stroll in the country. I really walk at a quick pace. I also think it's a good idea to get a set of those hand weights you can carry. This will build up your hands and arms. You might even consider getting some weights to wear around your ankles to increase the benefits of walking.

Walking is especially beneficial for people who are getting a touch of arthritis. It's important that you keep moving and maintain your flexibility.

Since I can't run, I also work out on a minitrampoline. Not only is it great exercise for my legs but it also helps tone the rest of my body. I know other players who ride bicycles—both stationary and racing bikes—whenever they get a chance. It helps build up their legs and their endurance, as well as keeping the pounds off, which will also help your legs from tiring on the back nine.

Saving Your Back

I know a lot of people are really excited about working out on weight machines to tone their bodies. That's fine, I guess, but I believe that you want supple muscles for golf, not bulky ones. That's why I prefer stretching exercises, especially for my back.

The first exercise I do calls for me to sit on the floor with my legs forming a V in front of me. I push my knees down flush to the floor, which helps stretch out my leg muscles. Then I simply alternate touching my toes. I'll stretch and touch my right hand to my left toe, then switch. The key is to keep those knees on the floor and really stretch. If you can't touch your toes at first, don't panic. Just take it slow and steady. It won't be long before your muscles have warmed up and stretched out.

After 10 minutes or so of the first exercise, I lie on my side with my arms stretched out over my head. I lift the top leg—right leg if I'm lying on my left side—up and down and then back and forth. This is really good for strengthening both my abdominal muscles and my back muscles. I also do this for 10 minutes or so, alternating between my right and left legs. At the same time I'm doing the leg lifts, I stretch my arms out, which stretches my shoulder and upper back muscles.

I do these exercises every day, but I make a point of doing them before I play. I don't want to get a good round started, only to have it ended by a sore back or pulled muscle.

EATING FOR FUN AND PROFIT

I'll let you in on a secret. I'm under contract with Nabisco Brands to be a member of Team Nabisco. I do outings for Nabisco. I wear Nabisco logos on my clothes. I have a Nabisco golf bag. What I should be doing for Nabisco is working as a taste tester. I am an expert on cookies and crackers and candy bars. And what I don't know, Ashley, Erinn, and Ray do.

In fact, if Nabisco made double bacon cheeseburgers, the company might satisfy my every culinary longing.

Sad to say, as much as I love all those good things, if I let myself go and ate all the foods I like, I might not be able to break 80, much less win tournaments.

For one thing, I wouldn't be in any kind of shape to play, and more important, I'd be so ashamed of how I looked that my game would disintegrate. I honestly believe that how you look is how you play. It all comes down to a matter of pride.

Beyond physical appearances, diet plays a key role in how well you can hope to play. If you are badly overweight or underweight, you won't have the strength to play. Even if you are in shape, the wrong foods can spell nothing but trouble ahead.

I never drank alcohol or smoked. I've never been a coffee drinker, seldom drink tea, and generally avoid soft drinks. I don't even bother with diet sodas as a rule. I'd rather drink fruit juice. All I really know about drugs is that you can't take them and play golf, which is about all I need to know. My gosh, I must have been a cheap date!

Without preaching, I think that if you're serious about really getting good at this game you should forget alcohol—at least before and during a round. People tell me they can have a beer and it doesn't hurt their game, but I have to wonder how good they could be without that beer. I'd even suggest skipping cocktails the night before a big match, since it takes a while for the alcohol to get out of your system.

Different people react differently to caffeine, but I have to believe it has an effect on your nerves, especially under pressure. The same goes for drinks with a lot of sugar in them.

When I'm on the course, I make it a point to drink a lot of water, particularly if it's very hot and humid. You must avoid becoming dehydrated. It's a good idea to try to drink a little water on every hole, rather than gulping down a lot of liquid every few holes. The idea is to keep your body on an even keel.

It's important to eat a big enough meal to provide plenty of strength, but I try to avoid large meals before a round, since it tends to make me groggy. I'll eat a good breakfast—fruit, an egg, some toast, and juice. If I get hungry or a little weak on the course—or if I feel my concentration slipping—I'll eat a few peanut butter crackers or some raisins. I ate a hot dog once during a round, and I thought I'd either die or shoot 80.

The important point is to eat and drink things that will help you maintain your strength and concentration. I think it will make a big difference in your game, but even if it makes just a small difference, it's the small things that often separate the rans from the also-rans.

Lopez File: Some of My Favorite Men

Over the years I've had a chance to play golf with a lot of the top players on the PGA Tour, either in exhibitions or in the team championship we play in the late fall. I've enjoyed it, and I've learned a lot from watching these guys play. Here are some quick impressions.

Curtis Strange

Photo courtesy of Robert Walker.

Curtis is my favorite. We won the J. C. Penney Mixed Team Championship in 1980. He and Ray are friends and love to fish and hunt together, which makes it nice.

When I first met Curtis, I thought he might be a little arrogant or conceited, but he's really just a nice, quiet, kind of reserved guy. His wife, Sarah, tells a funny story about first meeting him at a fraternity party at Wake Forest University. She saw Curtis sitting off in the corner by himself and of course was attracted to him because he's so good-looking. But she said he looked so shy that she really wanted to meet him.

Curtis, being Curtis, insists that he wasn't shy. He'd just had a couple beers and couldn't get out of the chair. I don't know how much of that is true, but it says a lot about Sarah and Curtis and their relationship. I'm very fond of them both.

Curtis is an outstanding athlete and a great player—and he's a great guy to have as a partner. He's very intense, but he doesn't take it out on his partner.

I remember playing one year in the mixed team. We came to the 54th hole tied for the lead. Curtis stiffed his approach, knocking it a foot from the hole. Naturally, he didn't bother taking out his putter . . . and naturally I missed the putt. I can't remember ever being so humiliated. Curtis had to walk over to his bag, get his putter, and knock in a three-inch putt. In front of a huge gallery. On national television. I wanted to die.

He was great about the whole thing, cheered me up, and the next day I came out and played great to make up for it. We went on to win the tournament. If we had lost by one shot . . . well, I'm not sure anyone is nice enough to forgive that.

Tom Kite

Tom Kite is a super guy. As much as he impresses me as a golfer, he impresses me even more as a gentleman.

People talk about the great players on the men's tour, and they mention Seve, Greg Norman, Jack Nicklaus, and so on. That's fine, but I don't know how anyone can leave Tom's name off the list. I think he's just an awesome golfer. He hits the ball so consistently well. I don't know if he ever has a bad ball-striking round by a normal player's standards. He's incredibly straight, but he also has all the shots. I admire him because he's so calm and so disciplined, especially under pressure. And he's so consistent. I guess he's easily the most consistent player on the PGA Tour, and for a professional golfer that's the ultimate compliment since that's what we all strive to achieve.

I think all young golfers—both male and female—would do well to pattern their games, and their lives, after Tom Kite. He's an outstanding role model on both counts.

Tom Watson

There's no doubt that Tom Watson will go down in the history books as one of the game's great champions and gentlemen. He symbolizes what is great in the game.

Tom is very intense on the golf course. He's always thinking about his swing, trying this and that. If I had to play like that, I'd be a mess, but then, I suppose he'd have a tough time with my approach to the game and the swing—so it all evens out.

Tom's been in a slump for a while. He hasn't won, and for a player of his standards and accomplishments, that's difficult to understand. Forget accepting a slump. No player worth his or her salt will ever do that.

People have to remember that Tom went head-to-head with Jack Nicklaus and then became the dominant player in the game for a long time. Getting on top is hard. Staying there is harder, and the pressure on Tom must have been enormous. On top of that, his son and daughter were growing up, and it's only natural to want to spend some precious time with your family instead of grinding on the practice tee. Sadly, as I've learned, the game isn't willing to share that easily.

Tom Watson will be back. And he'll be back with a vengeance. We haven't seen the last of Tom Watson. We may not have even seen the best of him yet.

Hale Irwin

Photo courtesy of Robert Walker.

When I think of Hale Irwin, I think of à guy who is the picture-perfect golf professional. Great swing. No-nonsense attitude. Has all the shots and knows how to win.

I had always heard what a great competitor Hale was. In fact, it always seemed, like a title. "Hale Irwin, Great Competitor." Like something you'd put on a business card.

I don't know what I expected when I first met him. I guess I thought he'd be this big, macho kind of guy. Instead, he kind of struck me as a businessman who has kept himself in good shape. When I watched him play, I was very impressed. He really thinks his way around a golf course. You never see him hit a stupid shot. He might not hit every shot perfectly—nobody does—but he never hits the *wrong* shot.

Hale has won two U.S. Opens, and I can see why. He plays well on difficult courses. He's very straight off the tee, so he avoids the rough. He plays smart shots, and he's mentally tough. That's a pretty good combination to bring to the Open. It's a pretty good combination to bring to any tournament.

Greg Norman

Photo courtesy of Robert Walker.

I really like Greg Norman. He's an exciting player to watch and a genuinely good guy.

I played an exhibition with him in England and was really impressed. He's such a gentleman and so competitive. He reminds me of Jack Nicklaus, and it doesn't surprise me to hear that they've become fast friends.

Like everyone else, I'm impressed with Greg's total game, but as an athlete I'm even more impressed with his attitude. When you realize that he's come within a shot of winning the U.S. Open, the Masters, and the PGA Championship, only to lose out—in two cases to freak shots—you could understand if he was bitter. Instead, he just resolves to go on to try to be the best player in the world.

It takes two things to come back from disappointments like that: confidence and courage. Greg Norman has shown the world that he has plenty of both, and the combination has earned him thousands of fans and admirers.

It's a sign of his determination that at the end of 1986, when he was Player of the Year, he sat down and took a hard look at his swing to see if there were any flaws. He found one and made the change.

All I can say to the other players on the PGA Tour is, "Good luck, guys." Can you imagine what will happen if he gets better?

Seve Ballesteros

Photo courtesy of Robert Walker.

By now almost every golfer has seen Seve Ballesteros hit shots that defy description, let alone belief. He's simply a genius with a club in his hand, and there's no doubt that he'll go down in history as one of the truly great champions.

I played with Seve in an exhibition one time, and later several of us went back to where he was staying. The hotel had those light switches that you press to turn on or off. Seve would stand across the room and pitch golf balls at the switches for practice.

And he rarely missed.

Seve is maybe the most charismatic player in the world right now, which I credit to his Spanish blood. He's just exciting to watch because he's so daring and he wears his emotions on his sleeve.

People argue about who the best player in the world is, but I'm not sure you can ever answer that question. I do know that if Seve played in this country he'd be a dominant player, particularly on the better golf courses.

Whether he plays here regularly or not, he's like Jones, Hogan, Snead, Palmer, Nicklaus, and a handful of other players in history. They are players you should go see if you ever get the chance. They are players of genius, and they are few and far between.

Fuzzy Zoeller

I'd have to say that next to Curtis, Fuzzy is my favorite player on the men's tour. He's very friendly, has a great personality, and genuinely likes people.

In fact, Fuzzy's personality is so strong and people like him so much that they often overlook what an outstanding player he is. He hits the ball a mile, can hit all the shots, and has a great touch around the greens. I mean, after all, nobody wins the Masters and the U.S. Open on jokes alone.

As impressive as his record is the fact that he's done this well with a very bad back. Yet there he is, week after week, having fun and playing good golf. Sometimes when I'm tempted to complain about some little ache or pain, I think of Fuzzy and put the thought right out of my head.

The thing I think everyone could learn from Fuzzy is his attitude. No matter how much pressure he's under, he never lets a bad shot bother him. He just goes on his way and hopes for a little better luck on the next shot. If that doesn't work out, he figures there are a lot worse ways to spend a few hours than out on the course. Now that's a good attitude.

Peter Jacobsen

Photo courtesy of Robert Walker.

How can this guy even play? Never mind that, how can he play as well as he does?

Peter is one of the funniest, craziest guys I've ever met. He is literally funny enough to make a career of it, and yet he's still one of the best players on tour. On top of that, he is genuinely one of the nicest guys in the world.

I know there are people who say that Peter might be too nice ever to be a great champion. I don't buy that. I do know that to win on tour you need to have a little bit of a split personality sometimes. When I'm coming down the stretch in a tournament, I can't be the same person that I can be when I'm playing with my daughters. I don't think that should come as a revelation to anyone.

But what I don't understand is what people expect from Peter. Should he go out and take "mean" pills? Should he go to a therapist for advice on being mean? And where do you write for a year's supply of killer instinct?

The point is that Peter is comfortable with who he is, and if he tried to change and become someone he's not, he'd be a mess.

It's a funny thing about being a golfer. People will try to tell you what's wrong with your swing. They'll try to tell you what's wrong with your equipment. Sometimes they'll even try to tell you what's wrong with your personality—even if it's a personality a lot of people love and treasure.

Lee Trevino

I left Lee Trevino for last, because I admire him so much as a player and because I can relate so well to him as a person.

Lee loves golf. I think he'd play every day just for the fun of it. He's been through a lot of ups and downs in his life, but he's never become cynical about the game. I think he's in a class by himself as a shotmaker. The only player that I could compare with him is Seve.

In this book I've talked about players who match their game to their personality. I think Lee Trevino might be the best example of that. He's an aggressive person, and when he's on his game there's no one more aggressive on the course.

We both came from similar backgrounds, growing up as Mexican-Americans in the Southwest. Lee grew up in a very poor family in Dallas. I wouldn't say we were poor, but there were times when the middle class looked like up to me. Heck, there were times in Roswell, New Mexico, when being middle class looked like the impossible dream.

Lee and I have never talked about this, but I'm sure that he must have know what discrimination was like when he was coming up. I was pretty much shielded from it, partially because the country's attitudes had changed and partially because my parents tried their best to protect me from it.

Still, I know what my parents went through, and I can pretty much imagine what it was like for Lee. Even now, I experience discrimination in funny ways. Maybe *funny* isn't the best word. . . .

Sometimes I'll go into a really nice shop, and the salespeople will either ignore me or hardly pay any attention to me. Then all of a sudden it will hit them that this isn't just another Mexican-American. This is Nancy Lopez, golfer and famous person.

It's amazing to see their change in attitude. Of course, by that time I'm out the door, because I believe strongly that people should be treated equally no matter who they are or what they do for a living.

I'm sure that all those little experiences are stored in the back of my mind someplace. And I'm sure that there's a little voice in my head saying, "Show them, show them," when I have a chance to win.

And you know what? I bet Lee Trevino hears the same little voice. Like I said before, it all comes down to pride.

12

Teaching a Kid to Play

Golf is the greatest game of them all.

You can play it by yourself and revel in the beauty, solitude, and peace that the game offers.

You can play it with your friends and enjoy the camaraderie, good-natured give-and-take, and thrill of competition.

You can play it when you're eight or when you're 80, and you'll learn something new every time out—about golf and maybe about yourself.

Those are just some of the reasons I love to see kids out on the golf course. I know how much I love the game and how much it has meant to me, and I just wish that more kids had the chance to experience just a fraction of the happiness I've had through golf. As a parent, I like to see kids playing golf because I've learned what my parents knew a long time ago: you very rarely see a kid get in trouble on a golf course.

Kids are the quickest studies in the game. They play by instinct and are great imitators. They don't get bogged down by theories, egos, self-doubts, or fears of failure. That's baggage we pick up as adults.

I never had to learn to love golf. I was fascinated by every aspect of the game. I was lucky because I had a talent for the game and because my parents took as much joy in my playing golf as I did.

I played in tournaments when I was ready to play in them—and when I wanted to. Mom and Dad never pushed me. If I won, that was great. If I lost, that was all right, too, because they understood that in this game you're going to lose more tournaments than you'll ever win.

Golf reinforced my self-image that I was somebody special, but it was the love and support I got at home that gave me that feeling to begin with. I never thought I was better than other people, only that I had been given a gift and it was up to me to do what I wanted with that gift.

As I got older I saw a lot of kids playing golf under an enormous handicap: their parents.

I'd see kids miss a shot, then steal a glance to get their parents' reaction. That reaction wasn't always supportive. Not by a long shot. That's a lot of pressure to play under.

I saw kids forced to play in tournaments where they were in over their heads. Competition is great, but you need to believe going in that you have a chance at making a good showing.

I saw kids who had to spend hours beating balls on the practice range when they really wanted to be with their friends, having a chance to enjoy being a kid. Spending hours on the practice tee is fine for pros. It's not fine for children whose parents want them to be pros, and the sooner the better. I can remember my father telling me that if I wanted to become good, I had to practice. I don't ever remember him telling me I had to go practice. The decision was up to me, and that's a big difference.

I've seen friends in college shattered, literally shaking in tears, because they had to call and tell their parents they'd had a bad tournament. They knew the lecture that was coming. They'd heard it a hundred times before.

I've seen kids trying to scratch out a living on the tour, and I know they don't have a chance. Worst of all, I know they know they don't have a chance, but they're too afraid to call it a day and get on with their life.

And maybe worst of all, I've seen a lot of kids burn out. I've seen them learn to hate the game, because they never had a chance to love it from the start.

I don't know if Ashley and Erinn will ever become great players. I don't even know if they'll be any good, but I do know that

they'll have a chance to enjoy the time they spend playing the game. That's what's important.

Here are a few rules I have for teaching kids golf my way. They worked pretty well for my parents. I hope they work for you.

1. Let children learn at their own speed—you can't force kids to have fun. Let them play or practice as much as they want, and then let them go do other stuff.

2. Teach them the rules—I don't mean you need to beat the rulebook into their heads, but you should tell them what's expected of them on the golf course. Teach them the proper etiquette. It will make life easier for everyone involved.

3. Expose them to good golf—if there's a tournament in the area, ask them if they'd like to go. Don't take them kicking and screaming, but give them the chance.

4. Start slow—I learned to play with a 4-wood that belonged to my mother. We shared her set in the beginning. I got the 4-wood, a ball, and a tee. She got the rest. I like this approach for two reasons. First, the best shotmakers—people like Trevino and Balles-

teros—learned to hit shots by playing with one club and improvising. Second, giving a child a bag full of clubs right at the start is a lot of pressure—plus it's a big investment if the child doesn't like the game.

5. Trust their instincts—I think the best approach is to show children a few fundamentals and then let them learn at their own pace. Once they ask for lessons, you'll know they're ready for them.

6. Take an interest—a lot of parents are more than happy to spend money on equipment and lessons for kids but are pretty cheap when it comes to spending some time with them. If you spend time with your kids on the course, you're giving them the clearest signal that you believe their golf is important to you.

7. Be a friend, not a critic—golf is hard enough without people always telling you what you're doing wrong. If you want to offer suggestions, do it gently. Better yet, wait for them to ask for help.

8. Tournaments can wait—I love competition, and I think playing in tournaments is the best way to improve, but I was never forced to play in tournaments. When I felt I was good enough to play with the other kids, I asked Mom and Dad if I could. But I had to feel I was ready. The last thing I wanted to be was embarrassed.

9. Let them caddie—many of the best golfers got their start as caddies. It's a good way to earn a decent amount of money, see a lot of golfers, both good and bad, and have a chance to play. Most clubs welcome, even encourage, girls to caddie these days. I've never understood why kids would rather work at a fast-food place than spend a few hours on the golf course, getting exercise and learning a game they can play all their lives. Plus, in many states, caddies are eligible for college scholarships.

10. Remember that golf is a game—golf is my job, and it's a job that's been very good to me; but when I was a child, my father constantly reminded me that it was a game. Even when I was winning tournaments, he kept reminding me that, win or lose, it was just a game. That was the best lesson of them all.

13

For Women Only: Some Special Tips on the Game

This is a great time to be a woman. We have more options that ever before. We can have a career. We can have a family. We can compete in sports, explore the arts. Do as much as we want or as little as we choose.

In a sense, I have the best of all worlds, since I have a family and a successful career playing a game that I've loved for as long as I can remember.

People often ask me how I manage to balance the many facets of my life, and to tell the truth, sometimes I think about it and it amazes me. I think one key is that I'm able to keep all the elements in perspective. As important as my golf is to me, my family is more important. And while my role as a wife and mother is very demanding and fulfilling, I still am able to maintain my identity as a golfer. In this regard, my life is "centered." Too often, I see people who have weighted their life to one extreme or another. They have a family, but no individual identity. Or they have a brilliant career, but no family to lend a perspective to day-to-day life.

Where does golf fit into this for most people? That's certainly a fair question. Most people who read this book are not going to carve out a career in the game, either as professionals or as top amateurs. But any sport or pastime can go a long way toward adding balance to your life.

Golf can be a good way to take your mind off the pressures of a career. It can be a formidable challenge or a way to relax. It can be a fine way to spend some time by yourself, working through the confusion and problems of daily life. It can be a great source of togetherness for the entire family.

Whatever form golf takes for you, the most important thing is that it should be fun. We all know there's enough stuff in this life that isn't fun. Why turn a game into a source of unhappiness?

I've tried to explain how I play golf, and I think that instruction is good for everyone, male or female, young or old. But in this chapter I'd like to cover a few areas that deal exclusively with women, since we are the fastest growing part of the game and to this point not much has been written to help women golfers.

EQUIPMENT

Here's my most important rule: If you are serious about this game, don't be afraid to spend some money. In golf, you get what you pay for. This game is difficult enough without trying to play with a bag full of wrenches. Take the time to go to a qualified professional and have yourself fitted to a good set. Make sure the grips are the right size, the shafts have the correct flex, and the clubs are the swing weight that is best for you. Also, keep in mind what I wrote earlier on equipment: unless you are unusually strong or talented, you can get along without the long irons for quite a while. Add an extra wedge or an extra fairway wood to your set instead.

Here's my second most important rule: do not, under any circumstances, buy clubs or balls that are pink. Do not buy equipment that has butterflies or flowers or any other silliness on it. There is a place for "cute" in golf, but it isn't in equipment. Look for clubs that have nice, clean lines. Avoid gimmicks. Give yourself every break you can.

DEALING WITH THE SUN

I like a nice tan as well as the next person, but the sun can do real damage. I'm not just talking about wrinkles. We've all seen the stories linking the sun's rays to skin cancer.

I always make it a point to wear a sunblock on my face and lips. I don't ever wear much makeup, and on the course I wear hardly any at all. I do put on a moisturizing cream to help my skin retain its moisture.

I almost always wear a visor, since this helps cut down my exposure to the sun. It's also a lot cooler. I'll never forget playing in real hot weather as a kid and being sick for a week with sunstroke. You need to have that happen only once to learn your lesson.

When you are playing in the heat, it's a good idea to wear light-colored, loose-fitting clothes. Natural fabrics like cotton breathe better and help keep you cooler. That's especially important in humidity, because you want to avoid having your clothes cling to your body.

In any kind of weather, I prefer to play in slacks or shorts. You should avoid playing in skirts or culottes that have a flap in front, since the flap can get in the way when you putt.

PLAYING WHEN YOU'RE PREGNANT

Golf is a great game to play when you are pregnant. It's a gentle form of exercise, and if you play regularly it can help you avoid gaining too much weight.

I played the tour during both my pregnancies. I stopped after about my fifth month in both cases. I have a tendency to put on a lot of weight when I'm pregnant, and since I have such bad feet to begin with, it made it too difficult to keep playing.

It was interesting trying to play when I was pregnant. My feet killed me, but I never putted better. I had an unbelievable sensitivity in my hands. It was kind of spooky.

My hormones went crazy during both pregnancies. I'm pretty emotional to begin with, but my feelings were on my sleeve the entire time. On the other hand, I had a wonderful sense of serenity during my pregnancies, and that's a nice feeling during a tournament.

Your diet becomes increasingly important when you're pregnant. Be sure to eat a good meal before you tee off and snack on fruit during the round to keep your energy up. Also, be sure to drink plenty of water during the round. You run a higher risk of dehydration when you're pregnant, so take the temperature into consideration before you play. I recommend that you forget playing in extreme heat.

You need to take all the precautions you normally would, especially in the final stages of your pregnancy. Avoid lifting heavy objects or other extremely stressful activities. You might also find it helps to take one more club for the shot and swing more easily. It's easier to get out of balance when you're carrying that extra weight.

Once the baby is born, take your time coming back. When Ashley was born, I tried to come back three weeks later. Bad idea. I didn't have the strength or stamina. I'd say two months is about right and maybe a little longer than that if you plan to nurse.

As I said, golf is a great way to exercise when you're pregnant, but like anything else, it requires a commonsense approach.

THE MENSTRUAL CYCLE

The menstrual cycle is a fact of life, and it affects all of us differently. Some women are lucky, and for them, their monthly period is little more than an inconvenience. For other women, it is torture—both mentally and physically.

On tour, you'll sometimes see a player shoot a series of high rounds after playing well for a stretch. It's a good chance that she's either reached her period or is in that stressful time just before her period. Either way, there's not much you can do about it.

My best advice is to know and trust your body. If you are a woman who has a difficult time physically and emotionally in your period, simply don't expect to get much out of your golf game during that time.

On the other hand, some women experience increased sensitivity during their periods. If that's the case with you, take advantage of it. You are one of the lucky few.

STAGES OF THE GAME

Once you've learned the fundamentals and become comfortable on the course, I think competition is the fastest way to improve. It forces you to concentrate harder and lets you lift your game to the next stage faster than by simply practicing.

Whether you are playing for a gift certificate or the U.S. Open trophy, the idea is to come away with a prize. There are people who say that winning isn't important to them, but I don't think they are telling the truth. I know that for me the thrill of winning is the greatest high. When I win a tournament, it stays with me for days afterward, especially when I can share the happiness with my family.

I think the key to competition is finding the right level. When I was a teenager, I won all the major amateur tournaments in New Mexico. People were trying to convince me to try the tour, but I had played in the Open since I was 15, and I knew I wasn't ready. The tour is no place for a girl to grow into a woman.

I went off to college, and that competition was fine for a while. But as I got older and better, I wasn't being challenged, and my game wasn't going anywhere. It was time to take my game to a higher level, the tour. Once I got there, the challenge was to win, then win again, and then win a major. The key to becoming a champion is to keep raising your goals.

Your current goal might not be to win on the tour. If you are just starting out, it might be to qualify for a club tournament, even at the lowest flight. Once you've done well in that flight, set your sights on moving up to tougher competition. As my dad always told me, keep your eyes on the horizon and your feet on the ground. That way you'll never get stuck in the mud.

14

Nancy's Pro-Am Package

I've lost track of how many pro-ams and outings I've played in, but the figure must be in the thousands. I really enjoy them. The people are so friendly, and even if the golf might not be world class, it's given me a chance to see probably every mistake it's possible to make in the game. That will come in handy when it comes time for me to give advice to Ashley and Erinn. It's already helped when I play with Ray.

People have been so good to me in golf. This final chapter is my way of giving something back. It's the 10 tips I'd like to be able to give personally to everyone who has ever cheered for me, or asked for my autograph or picture, or been with me in both the good and bad times. All of you mean more to me than I could ever express.

1. Have Some Fun

I play this game for a living, and I've had my share of bad days. But if I ever got to the point where golf wasn't fun, I'd just say good-bye. That's why I don't understand people who approach a round of golf as if it was a death march. Relax. Lighten up. Do your best, one shot at a time, and then move on. Remember that golf is just a game—and it's a game we're lucky to have the chance to play. There are a lot of people on this earth who aren't nearly so blessed.

2. *Get Some Good Equipment*

I like to see everyone get every break possible. Golf is a great game, but it is a difficult game to master, especially if you have the wrong equipment. Nobody is good enough to play well with bad clubs. Nobody.

3. *Slow Down*

I know that everyone lives at a different speed and that my slow tempo isn't right for everyone. Still, I honestly believe that if most people would cut their swing speeds in half, they'd be 100 percent better. The truth is, I see a lot of golfers with small errors in their swings that become catastrophes because they swing at breakneck speed.

Byron Nelson once said you can't stand too close to the ball. I say you can't swing too slowly. I dare you to try.

4. *Take Enough Club*

The great Bobby Jones had a secret. Under pressure, he always took one club more than he thought he needed, then made a nice smooth swing. This prevented him from overswinging and also ensured that he'd get the ball to the hole.

Sad to say, too often I see my amateur friends take just the opposite approach. They plan to hit their perfect shot every time—and wind up short almost as often. Do yourself a favor and take this test. Keep a record of your approach shots for five rounds. At the end, add up how many times you were short of the target, how many times you were right on the target, and how many times you were long. I think you'll be surprised. And I think you'll be reaching for one more club in the future.

5. Be Prepared

The Scouts were on to something when they chose this motto. I can't count the times I see my pro-am partners arrive flustered and unprepared, and they stay that way throughout the round. If you don't have time to gather your thoughts and emotions, you don't have a chance of playing good golf.

6. Warm Up First

Golf is a tough game, and the golf swing is a complicated motion. If you don't warm up before a round, you'll spend the first three or four holes trying to find a swing that works. By that time, you've made so many bad swings and mistakes that your score—and your patience—is shot. And it's nobody's fault but your own.

7. Find a Teacher

My father taught me how to play, but I suggest you find a good professional who will teach you a swing that's suited to your body and ability. Once you've found such a pro, stick with him or her. And avoid taking advice from well-meaning friends. As they say, free advice is worth about what you pay for it.

8. Watch the Ball

I don't just mean when you're hitting it. I see people hit a bad shot and then go crazy. There should be a two-stroke penalty for temporary insanity. Follow the ball into the trouble, and you won't lose as many balls. Follow a shot that runs past the hole, and you'll have a better idea of the putt you have coming back. Again, the idea is to give yourself every possible edge.

9. Take Your Medicine

Look, you have to realize you are going to make mistakes. Golf is a game of misses. When you get into trouble, get back into play in the safest way possible. Don't turn a one-shot mistake into a nightmare.

10. Learn the Rules of Etiquette

Golf is a game for ladies and gentlemen. That makes it special and sets it apart from other games where the rules are bent and everyone winks at boorish behavior. Even the best player won't be very popular if he or she violates the rules and etiquette of the game. Here are some basic ground rules:

- Don't step on a fellow player's line.
- Be careful to replace divots, ball marks, and spike marks, but remember that it's a violation of the rules to fix spike marks on your line prior to putting.
- Play in turn and be ready to play when it is your turn.
- Be still and quiet when your fellow golfer is hitting—and try to stay out of his or her line of sight.
- Congratulate a player on a good shot and pretend you didn't see a bad one.
- Keep your advice to yourself.
- Rake and smooth a trap after you've played.
- Treat your fellow players the way you'd like to be treated.

Index